"America needs citizens to extend the compassion of our country to every part of the world. So we will renew the promise of the Peace Corps, double its volunteers over the next five years and ask it to join a new effort to encourage development and education and opportunity in the world."

President George W. Bush
State of the Union Address
Washington, D.C. · January 29, 2002

Peace Corps
The Great Adventure

D0003662

OUACHITA TECHNICAL COLLEGE

Peace Corps
The Paul D. Coverdell Peace Corps Headquarters
1111 20th Street, NW · Washington, DC 20526
www.peacecorps.gov · 1.800.424.8580

Peace Corps: The Great Adventure

First printing: September 1997
Second printing (revised): March 1999
Third printing (revised): August 2002

Library of Congress Catalog No. 97-68135
ISBN 0-9644472-5-8

**For more information about the Peace Corps
please call 1.800.424.8580 or
visit our Web site at www.peacecorps.gov**

Contents

Renewing the Peace Corps' Promise

By Gaddi H. Vasquez

As the United States faced a season of unparalleled adversity, President George W. Bush envisioned our country "looking into a mirror and seeing our better selves." Americans were presented with a unique opportunity to reach out to people around the world, and show them the very best the United States has to offer. President Bush issued a call for every American to commit at least two years—4,000 hours over a lifetime—to the service of neighbors and nation. When called to serve, Americans respond. Within weeks, thousands turned to the Peace Corps for the opportunity to do good in the world.

Doing good in the world is a concept on which the Peace Corps was built. Since 1961, 165,000 Peace Corps Volunteers have done just that, turning their caring and compassion into action in 136 nations around the globe. Whether by teaching children, helping prevent environmental damage, working with farmers to improve their crops, educating people about HIV/AIDS, creating economic opportunity or bridging the digital divide, Peace Corps Volunteers reach out to the poorest of the poor with skills and spirit. Men and women of all ages, backgrounds and beliefs make up the Peace Corps, and show the rich diversity of America to the people with whom they live and work.

And now, the Peace Corps has been called upon to renew its promise and increase the number of volunteers serving abroad. If you have ever thought about learning a new language, embarking on an adventure, and sharing your skills with those in need, there has never been a more dynamic time to become a citizen of the world. Take some time to read through this collection of stories written by returned volunteers and learn for yourself how serving as a Peace Corps Volunteer can change your life. Journey to Paraguay where volunteer Rachel Peña took a bite out of a broccoli tortilla and learned that small steps add up to big results. Or visit Robert Soderstrom in Papua New Guinea where his fellow villagers set a new standard of generosity. Or join Dorothy Sales in Ukraine as she witnesses her adopted country crossing from one economic system to another.

Volunteers do more than transfer skills to their neighbors in developing nations. They are cultural ambassadors to and from their host countries. Volunteers spend two years learning about their adopted communities, speaking the local language, embracing the culture, and understanding their new friends with a depth few travelers ever could. But once their two years are finished, their service is not over. Returning to the United States, Volunteers are called upon to bring back the lessons they learned abroad, and teach others about the land they learned to love while away.

Peace Corps Volunteers serve goals larger than themselves: tolerance, understanding, humanity, self-sacrifice, kindness. As we face the challenges of this new millennium, it has never been more imperative to renew the promise of the Peace Corps.

Gaddi Vasquez is the 16th director of the Peace Corps.

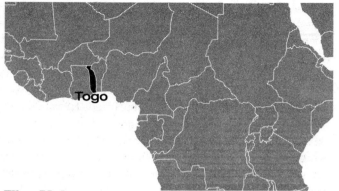

The Volunteer

by Jody Olsen

The car was covered with mud as we pulled into the African village. We had driven for three hours over unpaved roads from the Atlantic coast, passing through countless groves of palm trees and neat family compounds, past roadside markets and lovingly tended gardens and farming plots. The young woman beside me was a Peace Corps Volunteer, tense but consumed by a sense of anticipation. Since she had learned nine months earlier that she would be assigned to Togo, she had imagined this moment. In this village of five hundred, she would spend the next two years teaching health in the local primary school.

When we brought the car to a stop in the village center, a few people came near, smiled a welcome, and pointed to her new home, a two-room mud-brick hut with a thatched roof, surrounded by a neat fence of dried grass. Children peered shyly at her from behind the fences of their own houses as she moved in her baggage. Thus another Peace Corps adventure began.

I recalled at that moment, and I often think of it still, the start of my own Peace Corps adventure, when, over thirty years ago, I first saw my town in Tunisia. It was at night, and I was confronted with high walls and veiled women. Since that day, part of my identity has been fixed to that town, and to the Peace Corps. Not far away from my site, a group of Americans from the Agency for International Development worked as agricultural specialists, retreating each evening into large houses to resume their American ways. It was apparent to me that their technical competence far exceeded my own. My own self-esteem was to come from being part of the town itself, and of its caring people.

One of my responsibilities was to teach child nutrition, using Dr. Spock's Baby and Child Care, as it was the only book I had available. I remember an early lecture that I had worked so hard to prepare, on what to do for diarrhea. After I had proudly presented my lesson, an older mother raised her hand and said succinctly, "Give the child rice." I realized that there was a basic wisdom in that community, unsophisticated as it may have been, which I would have to learn to appreciate before I could really teach and be useful.

I am still not sure what I brought to my Tunisian community in the two years I lived there, though I did my best to teach English and family planning, and convey some modern notions of child nutrition. But I have a pretty good idea of what my town brought to me. Twelve years after I left, I went back for a visit, and the family I lived with embraced me as if we had never been separated. My own love for this family even today is as strong as for my family in the United States. In seeing my Tunisian family again,

I understood and appreciated how I had grown, and how much I had learned from them, while I was a part of a very special people.

So I knew what the young Volunteer was feeling as she reached her village in Togo, where I was then the Peace Corps' country director. I wondered what I could tell her to make her task easier. How could I share my own experiences with her? She had done well in training, but I knew formal training could only help her begin. The Peace Corps adventure is such a personal thing that each Volunteer must handle it with the resources of a private, internal spiritual reservoir. It eludes generalizations, textbooks, even words.

I knew from my own experience that the Peace Corps was an adventure based not just on exposure to unfamiliar geography and cultures. That was the easy part. In my own case, the more important exposure was to a segment of my own psyche that I had not previously known. What excited me most as a new Volunteer was the challenge of keeping an open mind, of trying out what I had never tried, of resisting the temptation to measure my experiences against what I had done before and was comfortable with, and of adjusting to a psychological insecurity brought on by the requirement to respond to a constant intrusion of the unfamiliar.

In time, the pride I took in myself as a Volunteer was in knowing I had the ability and the self-confidence to cope not just with the different, but with the unusual, knowing I could survive. At one point during my first year I wanted to stay in bed to keep away from all the differences, and I got up at six every morning in the cold and did exercises just to force myself to get going. But I made it, and life became better and better. I knew I could give the young Volunteer in Togo a few technical tips. But to assimilate into the life of her village, she was on her own. That is the experience that makes the Peace Corps special.

People in the Peace Corps have given a great deal of thought to the question of what makes a good Volunteer, without ever settling on an answer. Aside from self-confidence, the Volunteer must have common sense and a feeling for what is practical. I also think that a Volunteer cannot succeed without being idealistic. As much as anything, Volunteers must want to make things better in the community to which they are assigned. But, in equal measure, the Volunteer must also have patience, a commodity often in short supply among Americans, especially the young ones.

In most communities in the developing world, the same work patterns have been in place for generations, and Volunteers are likely to be dismayed at the desultory pace of change. Peace Corps Volunteers usually arrive feeling that two years is all the time they have to make a difference, and that every day counts. Characteristically, they go through a low period, after the initial exhilaration but before they have really mastered either the local language or the customs, when they wonder whether what they do really matters. After that, they begin building friendships, while acquiring a sense of what is possible and what is not. Finally, they feel a part of the community and its reality, and stop worrying about what they cannot do. The best of the Volunteers know how to make time pass in a positive way while they are waiting for events to happen. They are dogged, without being impatient.

But Volunteers must also know how to communicate their care and concern. They must know how to establish a trust between themselves and their community. In practice, they must know how to listen and how to detect differences between their own values and those of the community. Furthermore, they must be tolerant of these differences, accepting them as a base from which they may then introduce new ideas to make the community's life better. The Volunteer who sees virtue in introducing oxen for farming, new vegetables for family gardens, or inoculations for child health must frame the proposal in a way the community understands and can accept. The success rate is low for new ideas that offend old values. Volunteers must be able to put aside their own cultural system to work in another. In its forty years of experience, the Peace Corps has learned that this is not a capacity given to every Volunteer.

What explains why an American will volunteer to serve two years away from family and home, often in some physical discomfort, at no pay, frequently in conditions of considerable loneliness? It is a question routinely asked by the developing world whom Peace Corps Volunteers serve. In some cases, the question reflects suspicion. Some local people simply cannot believe that Volunteers would willingly give up American comforts. Although they may love the Peace Corps Volunteers who have come to their community, they are bewildered because they consider estrangement from family and home the worst imaginable punishment.

I specifically remember wanting to join the Peace Corps long before I could give it a rationale. I wanted to go to another country, live in a new environment, test myself on the unfamiliar terms that I knew I would encounter. I knew I wanted to "make a difference," a notion that seems to be a recurring theme among Peace Corps recruits. Who knows where this motivation comes from? In one way or another almost every Volunteer has it, combining a fundamental idealism with a practical objective.

For some, the motivation is simple curiosity, the desire to discover another country, experience its food, dress, customs, language. The Peace Corps is, after all, an exposure to the unfamiliar and, to a degree, the unpredictable. The presence of this objective seems to explain why the more exotic countries that the Peace Corps serves, those whose cultures are most far removed from our own, are traditionally those most sought after by Volunteers for assignment.

The practical counterpart of this idealism is the prospect, apparently entertained by increasing numbers of Volunteers, of using the Peace Corps experience as a springboard into an international career. Forty years ago, this prospect was absent, because there was no precedent, but international organizations have since learned to appreciate the attributes that Peace Corps Volunteers possess. Returned Volunteers are recognized as having a unique sensitivity to other ways of life and other cultures, and they rate highly compared with other Americans for their language ability. Peace Corps Volunteers, after all, are trained and they work in some two hundred languages. It is no exaggeration, furthermore, to say that the energy and adaptability of the Volunteer working abroad have become legendary.

Prospective Volunteers also see the Peace Corps as the opening to careers other than international. Graduates of the social sciences and the humanities often consider the Peace Corps a way to spend two useful years while they define their life goals. The Peace Corps is virtually unsurpassed in teaching the use of a foreign language. It has proven important to Volunteers in learning or sharpening skills in agriculture, forestry, public health, architecture, and engineering. Many returned Volunteers build upon their foreign experience to go into higher education, government service, and even electoral politics. Getting away, having time to think, serving while making personal decisions, and absorbing the meaning of new experiences have all become reasons for joining the Peace Corps.

Historically, the Peace Corps has tended to typecast women in their assignments. Men were generally given jobs in agriculture or construction; women were assigned to teaching or social work. Some time ago, however, this began to change. It is true that most developing world communities expect men to do the work in forestry or fisheries or in building water systems, but it seems likely that the involvement of women in this work has had a positive impact, not only on women in the developing world but on development itself.

When I went back a year later to the village where I had left the young health education Volunteer, I found her in her hut with two Togolese "sisters" by her side, playing a flute sonata. She was waiting for me with a special Togolese meal, jointly prepared with her family. Afterward, she excitedly took me on a tour of her village, calling to each person by name. She also described to me the special village rituals and traditions, achieved only by knowing the language. She talked of health issues and of the new well she and the village had just found the money to build. It would be completed before she left.

In her first year she had struggled, had questioned her purpose, had wondered why things moved so slowly. She had received some discouraging letters from home and had cried a little. But now she was happy, was learning, and more important to her, knew she was making a difference, at least to the families near her. After completing her tour in Togo, she came home to make new decisions about what really mattered in her life. She typified the Peace Corps experience, one we all share. It ties all of us together, no matter when or where we have served.

Jody Olsen *(Tunisia 1966-1968) taught English as a Volunteer in Sousse, Tunisia. Jody is a graduate of the University of Utah and received a master's degree in social work and Ph.D. from the University of Maryland. She was the executive director of the Council for International Exchange of Scholars, the organization responsible for managing the Fulbright Scholar program. Olsen came to the Peace Corps from the Academy for Educational Development in Washington, D.C. She was nominated by President George W. Bush and sworn in as deputy director of the Peace Corps on February 15, 2002.*

Ukraine

Adventures in Economics

by Dorothy Sales

"Why in the world would you do that?" I let the question hang in the air for a moment, and waited for the one that always followed.

"Won't that set back your career?"

They were questions I'd been asked several times since I'd decided to leave the business world for the real world and join the Peace Corps.

And they were questions that, perhaps naively, I thought had obvious answers. I had never considered that I was giving up anything by joining the Peace Corps. I had always thought of it in terms of what I was gaining. In addition to being a chance to make a difference in someone's life, I saw the Peace Corps as an opportunity to expand my skills, to gain experience, to challenge myself.

Joining the Peace Corps was something I'd always wanted to do. I can still remember seeing Peace Corps commercials as a child. As a teenager, I talked with some people who had served as Volunteers and it made a lasting impression on me. In college, my roommate served in Honduras for two years.

I had considered it many times, but as is often the case, life got in the way. After graduating from college with an economics degree, I stepped right onto the corporate ladder—first as a marketing representative in Boston, then as a fundraiser for a small college and prep school.

Finally, after eight years in the business world, I sent in my Peace Corps application. I never had a second thought, especially after I found out that I would be serving as a business Volunteer in Ukraine. It was an opportunity to help people build a free-market economy out of the wreckage of communism. It was an opportunity to be a part of a historic transition.

Before I knew it, I was living in a Soviet-era apartment building with no water or electricity at times, no air-conditioning in the hot and humid summers, and occasionally no heat in the sub-zero winters.

My job at the International Management Institute was to teach business communications and advise the marketing department. I also set up a new career placement center to help students find jobs after graduation.

In some ways, the job was very similar to working in America. I dressed much like I did back in Boston and used my laptop at home to prepare for the next day's class. But there were exciting changes going on that made it much different.

The country was in the middle of drafting a new constitution, establishing a new currency, and opening its first stock market. To witness the foundation of an economy being built and to be a small part of it is an experience few will ever have, and one that was not lost on me. Each day, I found myself learning nearly as much as my students. I shared the excitement and eagerness in the classroom as students embraced the spirit of free enterprise. They wanted to learn how free markets work, how to compete within them, both at home and abroad, and they worked hard to provide themselves with a framework for a better job, a better way of life.

There were many questions as they crossed the bridge from one economic system to another. What could they take with them? What experience would be relevant in the new economy? How could they apply the skills they had? These were challenges I helped them address. And often I think I felt more satisfaction than they did when they overcame the challenges. I know whenever I look back on it, I feel like I benefited more from the experience.

I know I discovered skills that I didn't know I had, I developed the ones that I did, and I gained experience that will help me for the rest of my career.

Often, when I tell people about all that I brought back from my Peace Corps experience, they say, "What a great boost to your career."

And I let the statement hang in the air for a moment, and wait for the one that always follows.

"I wish I'd done that."

Dorothy Sales *(Ukraine 1995-1997) served as a business development advisor in the city of Lugansk and the capital city of Kiev. Sales has a B.A. in economics from Trinity College in Connecticut. She is currently the coordinator of the United Nations Volunteer Program at the Peace Corps in Washington, D.C.*

Paraguay

A Taste of Success

by Rachel Peña

Tranquilo. All 32 of you will fit on this 15-passenger bus. *Tranquilo.* You'll learn Spanish and Guaraní in 90 days.

Tranquilo. This isn't even close to as hot as it gets here. Be *tranquilo.* Be patient. Relax. Take it easy.

I had come to Paraguay with big plans. I had goals. I had an agenda. I had specifically defined how I would measure my success. I had trouble being *tranquilo.*

Perhaps it's part of growing up in America, perhaps it's just me, but patience was a virtue I'd always had trouble understanding. And now, as I prepared for my Peace Corps service in Paraguay, I was becoming more confused than ever. I thought we were here to help. I thought we were here to make a difference. I didn't think we were here to relax.

And yet, every time I turned around: You'll learn Spanish and Guaraní in the next fourteen days.

Tranquilo. It gets much hotter than this.

Tranquilo. Tranquilo. Tranquilo.

I can't tell you how many times I heard that word during the three months of training. From trainers, from bus drivers, from my host family. In cafes, in the market, in the health center. And always, it was delivered with a calmness and a smile.

At the end of the three months of training I couldn't wait to get to my site. At last, I could get started. I could begin doing all the things that I had told myself I would accomplish.

My assignment was rural health education. The job involved a variety of basic but important work. I visited schools to teach children about the importance of brushing their teeth and eating healthy foods. I worked with women to educate them about the dangers of cervical cancer. I worked with a Paraguayan nurse to organize and run Pap campaigns. I also started a community garden with some teachers and their students. I joined other Peace Corps Volunteers and local Paraguayans to build sanitary latrines. I worked with the community to help establish a health clinic.

I was doing stuff. I was accomplishing things, but I couldn't help but feel I could be doing more. If it wasn't for *tranquilo*.

Tranquilo. The supplies will get here.

Tranquilo. The pigs don't know that they are supposed to stay out of the garden.

Tranquilo. It's not that hot.

The work I was most proud of, and the best times I spent in Paraguay, involved the Mothers' Club, which I helped form soon after I reached my village. Once a week, we would meet at a different mother's house or sometimes at the river to do laundry and bathe while we talked and learned from one another. Those women soon became my family. They warmly welcomed me into their homes, where they treated me as a daughter, a sister, a granddaughter, and a friend.

Naturally, I always had an agenda for our club meetings. A topic for discussion. A list of things I wanted to accomplish. We would talk about ways to improve nutrition and their diets, breast-feeding, pregnancy, vaccinations, child survival, first aid, and just about anything else that was related to keeping moms and their kids healthy.

And, of course, my goal was to do more than simply talk with the women. I wanted to see results.

Tranquilo. Things cannot change overnight.

Tranquilo. More people will show up for your next workshop.

Tranquilo. We can talk about that later. Let's have some tea first.

I wanted to see that my community had the lowest rate of cervical cancer in all of Paraguay. I wanted the Ministry of Health to single out my village as the only community in Paraguay with absolutely no intestinal parasites. I wanted every family to change their diets completely to include vegetables like broccoli, which grew like crazy in the community, but none of the mothers knew how to prepare. And I wanted all of this now.

Tranquilo. You are trying too hard.

Tranquilo. You will learn Spanish and Guaraní yet.

Tranquilo. It gets much hotter.

Every week I would remind my friends in the Mothers' Club about, among other things, the many wonderful qualities of broccoli, including its nutritional value and its ease of preparation. Yet, for all my efforts, I felt like I was getting nowhere.

The Great Adventure

One day, about a year into my service, I was waiting for a bus to Asunción in front of my neighbor's house. It had rained a few days earlier and the roads were still muddy, so it looked as though the bus might never arrive. I paced back and forth and mumbled to myself.

Tranquilo. The bus will be here soon.

I paced back and forth some more. *Tranquilo,* I told myself, the bus will be here soon.

Finally, frustrated, I sat down heavily on the ground. A short while later I looked up to see little Maria Brizuela, the daughter of one of the women in my Mothers' Club.

Tranquilo. The bus will be here soon, she said.

I managed a slight smile and noticed that she was holding a plate of tortillas that her mother had sent. She sat down next to me and handed me one.

I took one bite and all my delusions of grandeur slipped away. I let go of my timeline and my rigid agenda. Suddenly the heat and the disappointments and the pigs in my garden and the times when nobody showed up for a workshop and the crowded buses and the total frustration with the slower pace were all worth it.

Maria Brizuela's mother had put broccoli in her tortillas.

Maria explained that her mother was cooking broccoli in lots of different foods. She said that her father was even learning to like it.

After a while, Maria returned down the dirt road, and I returned to waiting for the bus.

Tranquilo, I said to myself, it doesn't matter if the bus ever comes.

For *la familia* de Juan de Dios eats broccoli.

Rachel Peña *(Paraguay, 1994-1996) began her career with children and families as a health education Volunteer in*

Kera'y, Paraguay. Today, she is a child welfare worker in Oakland, California. She holds a B.S. in child development from Humboldt State University, and she is working toward a master's degree in social work at the University of California, Berkeley.

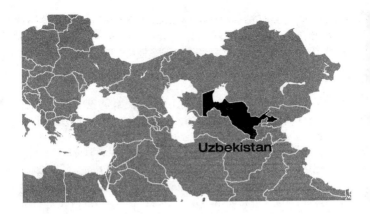

Uzbekistan

Doppas

by John Smart

Uzbekistan is one of those "stan" countries, a part of the former Soviet Union, a predominantly Muslim country with legendary cities of Samarkand and Bukhara, but it had been practically unvisited by tourists for over a hundred years. I had no idea what to expect there as a Peace Corps Volunteer, and nobody could tell me much either.

At age 56, I had traveled the globe extensively on business and pleasure, and I felt up to anything. Besides, as it turned out, there really was no way that anything or anyone could have prepared me for Uzbekistan.

The suffix "stan," incidentally, is Arabic for "the land of . . . ." Thus, Uzbekistan is "the land of the Uzbeks," and Afghanistan is "the land of the Afghans," and so forth. I had always wondered about that.

The countries of the former Soviet Union share a unique history and a peculiar uniformity of style. Except for some variations in language and food, casual observers wouldn't know if they were in Tashkent, the capital of Uzbekistan, Vilnius, Lithuania, or Vladivostok, in far eastern Russia. In fact, I met a young English woman while I was there who was studying Soviet architecture. She told me that she could look at an apartment block and tell in which year it was built, whether it was in Murmansk or Almaty or Baku, because that was the design that had come out of the Moscow architecture office that year.

A strange specialty, I thought.

But, beneath the surface, if you looked past the Soviet overlay, Uzbekistan was the most truly foreign place that I have ever been in my life. Once you got past the ugly, quasi-modern cities, and out into the old population centers and the villages, a wonderful view of an ancient culture came into focus.

The Uzbek people are primarily descended from the nomadic tribes that originated in the region called the Altai, in the mountains north of Mongolia, although they have been influenced by an incredible array of visitors over many centuries.

Samarkand and Bukhara were at about the halfway point of the ancient Silk Road, the trade route that Marco Polo traveled on his way to see the great Kublai Khan. And many others have been here as well: the Persians of ancient history, the Greeks with the young Alexander, the Mongols under Genghis Khan, the Tatars, Syrian traders, Turkish armies, Europeans, Chinese, and finally the Russians.

I was fortunate to be sent to lovely old Bukhara to spend my term of service. Bukhara and Samarkand officially celebrated their 2,500th birthdays while I was there, although all agreed that some organization or bureaucrat had rather arbitrarily settled on that particular age.

They're likely a lot older. On my first day in Bukhara, I was shown the very spot in the ancient citadel, "The Ark," where Alexander had wrestled a lion in 327 B.C.! I was overwhelmed by the history surrounding me, and remained so for the duration of my stay.

My duties as a Peace Corps Volunteer in Bukhara were twofold: I served as an advisor to the crafts community of the region, specifically in the marketing of their products to foreign buyers and tourists, and I taught economics in a high school, in English, to students for whom English was their third, fourth, or even fifth language.

Both of these tasks were challenging and highly rewarding. I had experience in marketing handcrafted merchandise, but I had never taught school before. I discovered that I loved teaching, and it has really had a major effect on my life. When I returned from the Peace Corps, I got involved as a tutor and substitute teacher in my hometown, where I spread the Peace Corps message every day.

The transition from life in the United States to that in a country like Uzbekistan, or, indeed, in most of the countries of the world where Peace Corps Volunteers serve, was certain to be somewhat unsettling. Learning to live within a Muslim society, indeed with a Muslim family where no one spoke English, was memorable, to say the least. I learned the Uzbek language, and came to know quite a lot about Islam from asking questions and from discreetly observing. During my stay, my Uzbek friends included me in their religious observances. I often attended the mosque with them for regular prayers, and I was invited to important events like weddings, circumcisions, and funerals. I was always made welcome, and I was grateful for the opportunity to learn far more than I taught.

I had an extraordinary opportunity to get to know the mufti of the Bukhara region. The mufti is the chief cleric in an area, as might be compared to a bishop in a Christian church. This man's name is Gauferjon, and I tutored his daughter in English. I spent many evenings in their home, eating delicious food, and having long conversations with the mufti. This was possible thanks to his daughter's excellent English translating skills.

Gauferjon was very well informed about how Islam is perceived in the West, and he was saddened that Westerners had gotten the impression from the news media that all Muslims threw rocks or bombs and caused civil disturbances. He likened it to a "what if" situation where his only knowledge of Christianity might be the news he received from Northern Ireland.

He also was a student of Islamic history, and told me about the Moorish period in Spain and the Ottoman Turkish Empire, and how these enlightened Muslims allowed all religions to flourish under their benevolent rule. He also felt that Islam had fallen behind the rest of the world in some ways, and longed for it to return to its real roots in the words of the Prophet, not influenced by the fanaticism that has unfortunately fueled its current reputation.

When I left Bukhara, Gauferjon gave me a *doppa,* the skullcap that is worn by all Muslim men. This particular *doppa* is white, with delicate white embroidery, and had been brought back from Mecca, when Gauferjon had made a hajj, or pilgrimage, to that holy city. It was a special gift for him to give me, and one that I will always treasure.

In fact, I will treasure all of my *doppas*. I have a lot of them, and there is a story behind them. I was given a traditional black and white Uzbek skullcap as a gift early in my stay, and, one very hot desert day, I put it on to walk into the old city of Bukhara. I didn't want to burn the top of my head again (the hair up there doesn't cover like it used to). I was, as I said, in my fifties, with gray hair and a gray beard, and, when I wore my *doppa,* people told me that I looked like a mullah or a wise elder.

I discovered that I enjoyed that image, so I wore a *doppa* every day for the rest of my stay in the country. My Uzbek friends, noticing this, started to give them to me, all sorts of *doppas,* embroidered silk *doppas,* hand-worked felt *doppas,* crocheted *doppas,* plain cotton "working man's" *doppas,* and all in a rainbow of colors. I ended up bringing home a nice collection.

There was a distinct advantage to being older in the culture of Central Asia. To these people, age and wisdom are assumed to be linked, and I was treated with respect and a certain deference, which I, of course, came to appreciate.

I tried to wear my *doppas* once in a while after I returned to the United States, but nobody at home told me that I looked like a wise elder. I miss that, a lot.

John Smart *(Uzbekistan 1995-1998) was a small-business development Volunteer in Bukhara, Uzbekistan. After his Peace Corps service was completed, he returned to his home-town of Park Falls, Wisconsin, to concentrate on volunteer work and being a substitute teacher.*

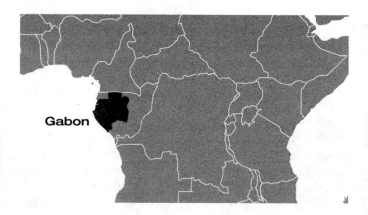

Gabon

The Fridge Factor

by Bonnie Black

If you live in equatorial Africa and you can't afford a refrigerator, you might as well kiss butter good-bye. And things like fresh milk and cheese and ice cream and cold drinks and last night's leftovers, too, just to name a few.

This is the latest lesson I'm learning here at my new post: how to live without a fridge, or, as one might put it in the lingua franca of this francophone central African country, *sans frigo.*

I can't say I wasn't warned. When my Peace Corps recruiter in New York learned I wanted to trade in my ten-year-old culinary career for a two-year stint teaching community health in Africa, he looked at me long and hard. "You won't be able to cook or eat the same way," he said. "The food will be very . . . ahh . . . different."

"No problem," I thought at the time. I waved the warning off. "With enough onions and garlic I can make anything taste good," I bragged.

What I didn't consider then, though, was the fridge factor. Such a simple, common, everyday appliance. Every kitchen I've ever known in my whole life has had one. A refrigerator, like a sink, stove, and oven, is what makes a kitchen a kitchen. First you wash, then cook, then keep the food from spoiling by refrigerating or freezing it. Why, a refrigerator is part of the very definition of a kitchen! Or at least that's what I used to think.

Now I can realize that for most of the people in the developing world, a refrigerator is a luxury item not even at the top of the list. There are four-wheel-drive cars and pickup trucks here in Lastoursville, a small town on the train line about two degrees south of the equator. And I see glimpses of television sets blaring in mud-wattle huts as I walk by. But refrigerators? Most people here—including me—cannot afford one.

How does this affect the way people shop, cook, and eat, I wondered when I first came face to face with the problem last month. What impact does it have on their overall diet and their health? If you can't keep food from spoiling here in the rain forest where bacteria and all sorts of insect life thrive, what foods do you choose?

I'm in the process of finding out. This is what I've learned so far:

- Forget leftovers. Some claim you can leave soups and stews, covered, on the kitchen counter overnight and boil them well the next day.
- Forget dairy products. I've actually come to like the full-cream tinned powdered milk here; and besides, I've always wanted to cut down on my consumption of butter and ice cream anyway.

- Forget ice cubes and cold drinks, and cold anything, for that matter. The sensation of having something cold in the mouth is now, at least *chez moi,* only a memory.

The trick, I've found, is to shop for fresh foods every day and cook only as much as you'll consume that day. For me this means walking about a mile to the market every morning to see what the ladies there have to offer.

"What is this, mama?" I ask an elderly African woman who has piles of leafy greens in front of her on a rough wooden table.

"Epinards," she tells me. But it doesn't look at all like the spinach I've always known and loved.

"How much?" I ask her.

"Cent francs," she says. I offer her the coin and we smile at each other as I struggle to scrunch the leaves into my net shoulder bag.

Every day I try to say a little something to each of the women there: What do you call this? How do you cook it? For how long? What does it taste like? As well as, How are you feeling today? What is your baby's name? Where were you yesterday? I missed you!

The ladies at the market have become my friends. Their warmth, their smiles, their greetings brighten my day in a way that no refrigerator ever could.

Just the other day, one of the mamas commented on the skirt I was wearing. It was a long, blue denim A-line skirt my daughter had given me for my birthday several years ago. The old woman said, half jokingly, half teasingly, "You could dance the tango in that skirt."

"Well, then, let's dance," I said. So she gamely got up from her wooden bench and we danced a little mock-tango —for everyone's enjoyment—right there, beside the piles of chili peppers and plantains.

Not having a fridge forces me to go to the market every day, but this is far from the hardship one might imagine. Every day I learn from these *marchandes de legumes* and enjoy experimenting with the produce I've brought back.

As soon as I get home I empty my net bag on the kitchen counter and proceed to create my *soupe du jour*—a hearty mélange of familiar and unfamiliar ingredients. Like life here in general, my soup each day is different from the one before. But the procedure I follow in making it is, like me, predictable: First I take onions and garlic …

Bonnie Black *(Gabon 1996-1998) was a community health Volunteer in Lastoursville, the heartland of Gabon. For many years prior to joining the Peace Corps, she was a chef and had her own catering business in New York City. She has a B.A. in literature and writing from Columbia University.*

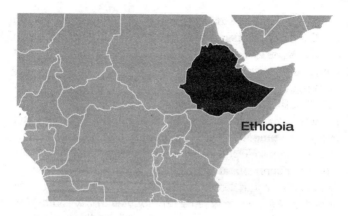

Ethiopia

So This Is Paris

by Kathleen Coskran

The year Detroit burned, I taught English and algebra in Dilla, Ethiopia. There were four of us *ferenjis (foreigner)* in Dilla that year. Doug, from Michigan, saved all the clippings from *The Christian Science Monitor* that his mother sent him about the riots and brought them out whenever a student asked him about his country.

He would unfold the pictures of burning buildings and say, "This is my home."

"He reads too much," Dick said. Dick didn't have time to read. He never missed a soccer, basketball, or volleyball game with the students or a chance to spend an hour at *Negussie Beit,* the only bar in Dilla with a refrigerator.

Our students called Claudie their mother because she stayed at school long after the sun went down to talk to them, help them with their homework, or give them advice. The day she bandaged Hamid's infected arm, he asked if she had ever been a Girl Scout.

"Yes, I was," she said.

"I thought so, miss, because you are always prepared."

The seventy-five students in 7-A, my homeroom, were impressed because I called the roll from memory every morning, Addiswork Bekele to Zeudi Memedin. They called us all the Peace Corps, but pronounced it "corpse."

We walked down to the post office after school on a clay road that sucked at our shoes in the rainy season and streaked our clothes with dust in the dry season. We passed kids shouting *"Ferenj!"* (foreigner) at us, stepped around sheep and goats crossing the main drag, stopped to admire the professional mourners in a funeral procession, paused so the water man rolling his massive barrel up the hill from the river wouldn't lose momentum. As the barrel rumbled past and the mourners took up their ululations again, and a six-year-old ran up, tagged him, and dashed back to his friends, Dick would spread his arms wide and say, "So this is Paris."

That year school began with a chalk shortage. One day I had used a piece of blue chalk down to only a shadow of color. Zelalem, from my sixth grade English class, asked me for the chalk after class, so I gave it to him, saying I wanted him to save it for me. Like the biblical parable of the man and his two talents, Zelalem gave me back twice as much chalk the next day. Somewhere he had found a grain of white chalk the same size as my spent blue piece. When I walked in the next morning, he opened his hand and proudly presented me with two precious specks of chalk for the class.

A few weeks later, in that same class, we were talking about capitalization. Each student gave me an example of a word that is always capitalized, easy words, such as

Ethiopia, Dilla, or their own name. I hesitated at Nasin Shaffi, the slowest boy in the school, who was often teased by the other students. I didn't want to embarrass him again. When I asked him for a proper noun, he stood up and mumbled something.

"What?" I said.

Nasin repeated what he had said, in clear, full tones: "Dag Hammerskjold."

On St. Patrick's Day, I explained my Irish heritage to the students in 7-A and the significance of the day. Abraham, the worst troublemaker in the school, raised his hand. "We should go outside, madam, to celebrate your holiday."

"No, that's not necessary," I said, but the students were already moving toward the door.

"Yes, yes, good idea," they said.

Tsegay Mekonnen, the class monitor, stood at the door to stop them. "No," he said. "It is her holy day. We must have five minutes of silent prayer." That was not what I had in mind, but they all went back to their seats and bowed their heads.

The first time I saw Tsegay in action, he was stepping across a desk in the back of my room with a switch in his hand to hit another boy who was talking out of turn. It was my first day at Atse Dawit School.

"Hey, stop that. What do you think you're doing?" I said.

Tsegay stood against the back wall with his arms folded across his blue shirt, watching me advance on him. "I am monitor," he said when I reached him.

"Who says you are monitor?" I asked. I was familiar with the monitor system of class discipline, didn't like it, and didn't want it in my classroom.

Tsegay shrugged, but the other students confirmed that he was the class monitor. I said the monitor should be elected by the class and proceeded to explain the democratic process, the duties of the monitor (no switches allowed), the responsibilities of the students to each other, to the monitor, and to their teachers. I then took nominations from the floor. They elected Ayelu Hailu.

Because not everybody was able to start school when they were six years old, the age range of my seventh graders was twelve to twenty-two. Ayelu was a slight twelve-year-old, the smallest boy in the class, meek and overwhelmed by his sudden elevation to high office. The students snickered when I announced the election results. I insisted that they respect Ayelu, affirmed my confidence in him, and said that his word would be law regarding areas of discipline. Ayelu took a deep breath, straightened his shoulders, and strutted to the back of the room where he could keep an eye on everybody. I resumed the math lesson.

He lasted four days before quitting.

The second time around, they elected Hamid. I was pleased. Most of the students had chiseled features, slight frames, and the red-brown skin of the highland Ethiopian, but Hamid's family had emigrated from the far west. He was an imposing figure, six feet tall with very dark skin. But his service as monitor was a day shorter than Ayelu's. I didn't understand why he was unsuccessful until much later, when I heard him called "the black one" and *shankalla* (slave).

I told the students that I was furious with them for electing two successive monitors whom they refused to respect.

"Tsegay is our monitor, madam," somebody said.

And so he was. Restored to office, he became an invaluable advisor for me, an inside operator. "Bekele is not sick,

OUACHITA TECHNICAL COLLEGE

madam. He have woman." Or "Kebede hates Hamid. Better move him." When I remember my class now, Tsegay's handsome face is always in the middle of the back row, his eyes roving over the rows of students. It was the end of the year before I persuaded him to give up the switch.

We had electricity from six p.m. to midnight most nights. I planned lessons and graded papers when the lights were on. After midnight, I sat up with a book, reading by candlelight in the dark kitchen. I savored each word of those delicious books. I also read *Time* cover to cover every week, including the sports and business sections; I read the listings of books published on the flyleaf of Penguin Library editions; I read the small print of ads in the English-language *Ethiopian Herald,* a weekly newspaper. I even read *The Fannie Farmer Cookbook* cover to cover. I knew nothing about cooking, having been raised by a mother who believed that packaged foods were the most profound scientific advance of the twentieth century.

There was not any processed food in Dilla. We could dependably buy only onions, bananas, and meat. Sometimes there was cabbage and carrots. Once there was eggplant. We could also get rice, but there were insects in it. We had to dump it on the table and scrape the rice into a bowl while killing the bugs and pushing them off to the side. Salt and spices were measured into cones of old newspaper when we bought them. The egg man delivered his tiny eggs wrapped in banana leaves. When we went to Addis Ababa, we bought oatmeal, canned margarine, tuna fish, powdered milk, and tins of vegetables. The tuna and vegetables were so precious that we allowed ourselves to eat them only on special occasions. In the end, we left two cans of beets, one of green beans, and one of corn for the next Volunteers. We wrote them a long letter, introducing them to our town, our kids, and our canned vegetables.

One day, Ato Mahari and Ato Hamare, the Amhara bankers, dropped by for tea and invited the four of us Volunteers on a picnic.

"Terrific," I said. "Do you want us to bring something?"

"Yes, of course, you women will cook, but we will hunt first. We will get partridges and two tiny antelope known as lesser kudu and have a picnic in the grand style," Ato Mahari said. Mahari and Hamare were as *ferenji* as we were in Dilla, where the people were either Sidominia or Derasse. The two of them, the four of us, plus Ato Aberra, a big man on the Coffee Board, and Ato Bekele, the school superintendent, formed the middle class of Dilla. A handful of local landowners and Negussie and Mohammed, who owned bars, were the upper class. Mahari's and Hamare's wives were shy, elegant women who didn't eat with us when we were invited to their houses. They would not be going with us on the grand picnic.

Claudie and I couldn't find a single reference to lesser kudu in *The Fannie Farmer Cookbook*. We approached Dick and Doug for help. They were sitting on their front porch with Tafesse, the third-grade teacher who lived with them. Dick had just come back from a soccer game and had a towel wrapped around his head to soak up the sweat. Doug was reading. Tafesse was smoking a cigarette.

"They expect us to cook," I said. "You have to help us."

Dick rubbed his head with the towel. Tafesse stubbed out his cigarette and grinned. Doug looked up from his book.

"You're the best cook," Claudie said to Doug. "You cook the kudu."

"Can't," he said. "Would be insulting to Mahari and Hamare. We are guests in their country and must obey their customs."

"It is clearly woman's work," Dick said.

I said, "Come on, you guys, this is serious."

They wouldn't help us, so Claudie and I concocted something we called "coleslaw," bought bread, and gathered up some spices.

The day of the picnic, Mahari did kill two of the tiny antelope known as lesser kudu. He skinned and bled them for roasting while Hamare built the fire and Claudie and I paced nervously.

"We've got these spices," I said. But in the end Mahari roasted the delicate kudu parts himself, without the spices, and we had our grand picnic in a grove of flat-topped acacia trees under the watchful eyes of local Derasse children.

Even the most remote town in Ethiopia has one or two Italian men who married Ethiopian women after World War II and stayed on to bake bread or make pasta. In Dilla, a man named Montenari ran a small bar and the only bakery. One Friday, Dick and I stopped at his bar just before midnight. The place was empty, he was ready to close, but he still had coffee, so he poured us some, and himself some, and sat with us. He did not speak English and only a little Amharic, and we spoke no Italian, so the three of us sat there in silence, this old Italian and two young Americans, drinking espresso in the middle of Ethiopia. At midnight, the lights went out. Montenari held his hand up and shook his head, insisting that we stay. He brought candles and more coffee. We sat with him a while longer and listened to the hyenas that began their eerie calls as soon as the lights went off.

When we finally left and walked home in the dark, Dick took my hand. "Yes," he said, "Paris is like this."

I had a party for the seventy-five students in my homeroom the week before we left Dilla for good. I made popcorn and bought bananas for refreshments, but I was stumped when it came to entertainment. Music was not a choice; our radio reception was too poor and I did not have a record player. The house was small, but I thought the kids could mingle and talk, eat a banana, and extend the party into the yard. But they wouldn't go outside. They filled one room. I tried to engage them in conversation, but they were politely monosyllabic. I offered the popcorn, but the easy laughter and conversation from the classroom were silenced by the solemnity of the occasion. The party in my house had made them mute.

Finally, Tsegay said, "Madam, can we dance?"

"Yes, of course. But where and to what music?"

"Don't worry, miss." Tsegay issued instructions to several of the students, took Addiswork's scarf, and stepped to the center of the room. Yakob found an empty patch of wall and drummed the mud plaster with the fingers and heel of his hand. Tsegay began moving in small circles in the middle of the room. The girls sang. Bekele clapped his hands in counterpoint to Yakob's drumming. Tsegay moved faster, holding the scarf taut between his hands, over his head, behind his back, then dropping an end, following it. Everybody sang, punctuating their songs with shouts and ululations.

They were of different tribes, different religions, but they knew what to do. When Tsegay finished, Addiswork took her scarf and stepped to the center of the room herself. Everybody sang and drummed as she began to move. My party was a success.

On our last day, we got up early to take the first bus to Addis Ababa. When I opened the back door in the pre-dawn light to go to the outhouse, I discovered Tsegay, Hamid, Zeudi, Ayelu, Mulugetta, Nasin, and Zelalen waiting in the yard. Dozens of students had gathered in the dark so they wouldn't miss our departure. They hovered around our two houses as we packed. They trailed us down the dirt roads of Dilla for the last time. They insisted on carrying our belongings to the bus. Tsegay presented me with a basket his mother had made. "So her name will be known in your country," he said. We got on the bus and waved until we couldn't see them anymore.

The road out of Dilla is a steep climb and the bus slows to a crawl at the last switchback. There is a point where the whole town looks like a map—four parallel streets, up from the river, bisected by paths, with the school at the high end and the bus park where clumps of our kids still waved at the low end. The four of us pressed against the windows for a last look.

"So this was Paris," Dick said softly.

"This was better," I said.

Kathleen Coskran *(Ethiopia 1965-1967) taught English and math in Dilla, Ethiopia, and spent two years in Kenya. Her book,* The High Price of Everything, *winner of a Minnesota Book Award in 1988, includes stories set in both Ethiopia and Kenya. She co-edited an anthology of travel stories written by women,* Tanzania on Tuesday. *She is the principal of Lake Country Montessori School in Minneapolis.*

**Papua
New Guinea**

A Single, Lucid Moment
by Robert Soderstrom

As the plane buzzed back over the mountains, it was now just us and the villagers of Maimafu. My wife, Kerry, and I were assigned to this village of 800 people in the Eastern Highlands Province of Papua New Guinea. It looked as if we were in for a true Indiana Jones adventure!

The mountains were dramatic and thick with rain forest. No roads had ever scarred them. We had loaded a four-seater plane with cargo (we would fly out every three months to resupply) and flew for thirty bumpy minutes southwest to the mountain ridges. From the plane, the village looked very much like a shoebox panorama from a grade school science project.

My wife and I were the first Peace Corps Volunteers ever in Maimafu. We had been greeted by a large group of beautiful people, all wearing gorgeous, curious smiles. Giggling, naked children hid behind trees during the trek down the mountain to our new home, and a lively entourage followed using their heads to carry our boxed supplies through the muddy trails. It was quickly becoming clear that we had just been adopted by a very large and unique family.

The basic culture of subsistence living had not been replaced; there were no cars, electricity, or telephones— just grass huts, large gardens, and a whole lot of rain forest. The women spent the day in the gardens planting, weeding, and harvesting. The men grew coffee, from which they generated their sole income of about $200 a year. The village had lived in harmony with its natural surroundings for millennia.

The villagers had built us a beautiful, bamboo-thatched hut on short stilts. Planted behind the house was a three-acre garden, carefully tended and ready to harvest.

Its bounty included corn, greens, tomatoes, beans, peanuts, onions, potatoes, and pineapples. To top it all off, the path to our new home was sprinkled with flower petals the day we arrived.

It quickly became clear that Maimafu was a preserved example of communal living. Men rallied to the building of a new home, the elderly worked and lived with their families, and mothers breast-fed their neighbors' children. In fact, the one parentless, Down's syndrome man in our village was fed, housed, and clothed by everyone; he would spend a few days with one family before happily wandering into work or play with the next.

It was when we had settled in that it happened. We were sitting in a circle on the ground with a large group of villagers to *"tok stori,"* Papua New Guinea's favorite pastime of "telling stories." I had passed around photos I had snapped back home in Chicago. A villager was staring intently at one of the photos. He had spotted two homeless men on a Michigan Avenue sidewalk with crude signs propped between their legs.

"Tupela man wokem wanem?" he asked. "What are these two men doing?"

I attempted to explain the concept of homelessness to the group, and the desire of these two men to get some food. Crowding around the photograph for a good stare, the villagers could not comprehend how the men became homeless, or why the passersby in the photo were so indifferent. They bombarded me with questions and I did my best to make sense of the two, ragged beggars in the midst of such glittering skyscrapers. I read from their questions and solemn mood that they had made an important observation—these two men must lack not only food and shelter but also a general sense of affection and purpose in their community.

Early the next morning, we were startled to hear a sharp rap at the door. Opening it, I was greeted by Moia, Kabarae, Kavalo, and Lemek. Kerry and I went out into the bright beautiful day. Each man gave us a pineapple. Moia spoke: "After you left last night, all of us men on the village council had a very big meeting. For a long, long time we discussed the two men in your picture. We have reached a conclusion and have a proposal for you."

"What could this possibly be?" we wondered.

"Please contact those two men as well as your government. Ask the government if they will fly those two men to Maimafu, just like they did for you. We have marked two spots of land where we will build houses for those two men, just like we built for you. Our men will build the houses and the women will plant the gardens to feed them."

They were offering to do what? I was stunned and overwhelmed. Their offer was bold and genuine. It was innocent and naïve. It was beautiful. And, like the twist of a kaleidoscope, my worldview had completely changed.

What does one say to such an offer? We stammered for a response and stumbled over explanations of difficult logistics, scarce money, and government bureaucracies. But the councilmen would not accept no for an answer. In their simple lives, it was impossible to comprehend that humanity was host to such an injustice. They wanted action.

The villagers were serious. They were offering everything they had. We reluctantly matched their enthusiasm with a few letters to America and long conversations with the village council. We toured the sites where the homes were to be built. We listened to the women discuss the type of gardens they would plant, which would even include coffee trees to generate a small income. And we answered numerous questions over time from villagers amazed with this foreign thing called "homelessness." The plan could not work, we told them. Their hearts sank, and I could see in their eyes that this dream would not die easily.

"Sori tru, sori tru we no inap wokem dospela samting," they told us. "We are sorry this can't happen." They clicked their tongues and shook their heads in disappointment.

Initially inspired by the episode, I began mulling questions over and over in my mind. Fetching water in the inkblack night and looking up the hill at our small hut, light from the lantern inside splitting the bamboo-thatched walls, I would think of the spiritual wealth of Maimafu and the material wealth of America: Can a community reach a balance of material wealth and spiritual wealth? Why do these two societies exhibit so much of one and not much of the other? Do those two ends interfere with each other? How much spiritual wealth can we have? How much material wealth do we need? How has the world evolved so that some people own mansions and others lack shoes? How many people have love in their souls but diseased water in their drinking cups?

The villagers worked with us on newer projects. And I discovered, like many Peace Corps Volunteers, that the world's purest form of brotherhood can often be found in the smallest of villages.

Robert Soderstrom *(Papua New Guinea 1996) was a community service Volunteer in Papua New Guinea. He has a B.S. in business administration.*

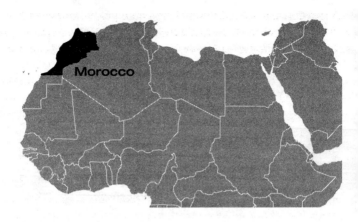

The Rhythm of Women

by Kathy Crabb

You must be patient and flexible. You must be patient and flexible. I heard that warning so many times during the Peace Corps application process and training that it would have become a mantra if I hadn't grown so sick of it. Okay, enough already, I'm flexible! I'm patient!

Now, more than a year has passed since I was sworn in as a Peace Corps Volunteer and assigned to Morocco. My patience and flexibility have been tested in every way imaginable, from transport that shows up a day late to co-workers who value paper pushing over useful action. I've learned that I'm not quite as patient, or as flexible, as I thought I was.

But I'm getting better. It's a matter of self-preservation. I must be patient and flexible to live and work in my little village in the High Atlas Mountains. Sometimes the road is washed out and transport doesn't run. Sometimes the social formalities of tea drinking take precedence over the things I feel need to get accomplished. My favorite example of just how patient and flexible I've become happened only today.

My best Moroccan friend, Fadma, promised she'd help me out with a survey I was conducting on home birthing practices in the region. Since she understands my American-accented Berber better than anyone, she said she'd help interpret between me and the women I wanted to interview. Our first stop was the home of Fadma's niece, Bzza.

Bzza wasn't home when we arrived, so her mother-in-law sent a younger sister out to find her and poured Fadma and me mint tea. She told us their neighbors were having a wedding that day—we could just hear the beat of the wedding drum through the thick, warm air—but no one had come by to invite them. Fadma sipped her tea, clucked, and muttered, "Shame, shame," under her breath.

After an hour or so of tea and complaining—and still no sign of Bzza—I started to wonder if I should come back another day. I could interview Fadma herself; she had a baby about six months ago. As I was about to get up and make my excuses, Bzza burst into the room. She accepted a glass of mint tea from her mother-in-law and began clucking over the wedding invitation. I thought, this can't go on much longer. A few more clucks and I make my move.

But the conversation didn't stop—it just blasted forward, full steam ahead, growing in volume and intensity, the women's hands flying back and forth, heads thrown back in half-bemusement, half-despair as all possible aspects of the offense were examined, hashed out, and argued over.

In the end I didn't interrupt. As Bzza was pouring the fourth round of tea and I was plotting my escape for the second time in an hour, a young neighbor woman appeared in the doorway. "Come and dance!" she shouted into the room. "What are you doing?! Come to the *ahaydous!*" (wedding dance). The women sprang up with eyes on fire.

"Yallah, Dunia!" Fadma shouted, as she pulled me up by the wrist. "Let's go!" We slipped into our shoes and half-strutted, half-danced out the door and over the rocky hillside to the neighbors' house. "We'll just stay for a bit," Fadma promised me as we entered the house. "Then we'll do the interview."

I nodded. Yeah, sure. Just looking at Fadma's eyes, the way her body perked up and started moving at the mention of the *ahaydous,* I could tell we weren't going anywhere anytime soon. I calculated how many days I had left to get these interviews done, how many interviews per day that meant.

I followed Fadma's lead, circling the room, grasping each woman's hand in turn, touching children's heads, asking about everybody's health, homes, families. There were perhaps thirty women and as many children in the room. Most sat on the floor, feet tucked under them, babies tied to their backs. Some ate *taam* (thick white gruel with melted rancid butter) and others sipped steaming glasses of mint tea. One woman was a blur of glass washing, tea brewing, tea pouring, tea passing. She fed frankincense into the *mijmar* from time to time to keep the air fragrant and festive. I squeezed in against the wall, and somebody passed me a spoon. I took a few hot bites of *taam.*

A girl in the corner started up a soft drumbeat and several women, prodding and pulling others along with them, rose to form two lines facing each other. They grinned and clapped to the rhythm of the drum, pressing their shoulders against their neighbors' shoulders. One woman started a high-pitched, wailing chant that kept time with the drum. The other women joined in and the volume grew.

"A good life for the bride and groom," they chanted. "Many children…good health…prosperity…." One row of women began the chant and the facing line echoed back; everyone stood still, chanted, clapped, and grinned. The late-afternoon sun filtered in, winding its way between the two lines, reflecting off the swirling incense smoke, off the silver spangles on the women's bright dresses.

Slowly, they began to move—one woman first, a slight move right, then a small move left, her neighbors picking up her signal in domino fashion until the entire line was inching back and forth. The facing line echoed their movements, chanted in return, everyone moving just slightly; but somehow with each move the entire group shifted a little to the right.

Staying in parallel lines, they moved around each other in full circles, a little faster now, and a little faster still. Each woman in her bright spangled dress became a sparkling part of the whole beating, swishing, chanting circle, clapping, stepping, breathing the thick frankincense, looking into each other's eyes and smiling widely.

The bride was not there; these were some of the women of her extended family. The bride is seen only twice during the three-day wedding festivities—once, fully and thickly veiled, dressed from head to foot in bright red and a great deal of clanking jewelry, on the long, slow parade through town. The second time, her face is uncovered but her eyes are closed as she is presented in the courtyard of her new home to members of both families. The parade and the presentation both feature an hour-long *ahaydous*, the drumming line of men and the echoing line of women. In the "co-ed" *ahaydous*, all the women but the leader keep their eyes closed, their faces down, their chants calm and quiet and even. They are shy, modest.

There was no modesty that afternoon. Someone pushed Fadma to the middle when the two lines degenerated into a ragged, pulsing circle. They tied a scarf around her hips and, with very little prodding, my best Moroccan friend shook her booty like a belly dancer in a B-movie. Fully clothed, she put on a sexier floor show than anything you could hope for at a strip bar in the United States. The rest of the room writhed and shouted, laughed and ululated, egging her on in boisterous, appreciative tones.

One octogenarian got really into it. She strutted over to the *mijmar* and flung the hem of her skirt over it to perfume her legs with frankincense smoke. She swiveled her hips back and forth for effect and pranced back to the *ahaydous*, hooting and grinning wickedly when she saw my eyes popping out.

The next time it started up, someone pulled me into the *ahaydous*. Wedged between Fadma and the risqué octogenarian, I clapped to the drumbeat and felt my heart pick up the rhythm, sensed the chants seeping into my body, kept my shoulders stiff and unmoving as my feet picked up the pattern of the slow shuffle. It could have been five minutes or five hours that we danced; it was entrancing, addicting, to become part of the rhythm and the movement of these women. Finally, with a fierce, high-pitched ululation, the drummer finished off with a flourish, a low collective shout went up, and somebody uttered a loud sigh. *"Igran!"* The fields. It was time to get to work, cut grass for the animals, pick potatoes for dinner.

"No, nooo, NOOOOOOOO!" someone protested.

"There's still time!" someone backed her up.

"Come on," a third chimed in, and the old frankin-censed woman hooted and rounded people up to keep dancing, keep dancing, keep dancing. A brief thought leaped through my mind about some vague job-related thing I was supposed to be doing, but I was pulled into the *ahaydous* again and found my legs moving in time with a dozen other women. The thought was gone. By the time three more calls went up to get to the fields, and three more protests beat them down, there was only half an hour of daylight left. Normally, women spend two hours each morning, and two again in the afternoon, working in the fields. There was a look of happy defiance, an unadulterated joy in every body, soul, and voice that no interview could have revealed.

This was my real work, I thought. Physical health is important, but today I found out what makes these women's hearts beat, what makes their eyes shine, their skin glow, their blood flow. This was my prize for being patient, my reward for being flexible. The work will get done. But in the meantime, pass the frankincense.

Kathy Crabb *(Morocco 1995-1997) was a maternal-child health Volunteer in M'semrir, which is located in Morocco's eastern High Atlas Mountains. She worked with local Berber women to improve home birthing practices, prenatal care, and recognition of risk factors during pregnancy and birth. She has a B.A. in politics from Mount Holyoke College.*

Guyana

Telling Time

by Katherine Jamieson

For two years I lived in a country with no seasons. We measured time by other means than falling leaves or snow, new buds on trees. There was a fresh breeze in the air, the ash of burned sugar cane floating in the window. There were times to go to work, times to stay home, an election, an eclipse; all of these differentiated the rising and setting of the same hot sun, and the appearance of a glowing moon and full set of stars. Rain would break the swelter like the fever of a child dissolves into sweat, and the whole city would breathe differently that day. Then the sun would come again and dry what had fallen, and could not last.

I came to this country with the expectation of seasons, and before I had woken to a blinding sun on Christmas, I imagined my yard littered with leaves, a chill in the air. It was here, in this place of twelve-hour days and twelve-hour nights, of weather and no seasons, that I learned to tell time. Telling time is like telling a story: The truth, the time, depends on the teller and the audience.

In Guyana, people will ask you, "Now is what time?" or, "Today is what day?" because they know the constants in life. There will always be "now" and "today," while the names we give them, 3:15 or August 8, are only names, and names that change.

My watch broke in my first few months; I had calendars, but the holidays changed with the moon. Without the time tellers I depended on, I realized, for the first time, that I was on my own.

My days and schedules shifted under the weight of unplanned, unused time, and I discovered that when time had no name, it became a broad expanse of life. Eventually, I learned to measure differently, to find my own names for seasons, without words or numbers. The poet Ted Hughes has written of this experience:

> I think of it
> As a kind of time that cannot pass,
> That I never used, so still possess.

I did not use this time either, I discovered it, and in so doing reminded myself of what I had so easily and quickly forgotten in a well-measured life. More importantly, I learned to answer the Guyanese questions that had confused me initially. I could say that now is when the frogs sing, and now is when the rain falls. Now is the howl of monkeys, the smell of curry stewing, the taste of mango pulled from a tree. And today, today is our understanding of being, our sense of ourselves as alive. It is without season or name, sun or rain; it is how we can live wherever we are and grow and grow and grow.

Katherine Jamieson *(Guyana 1996-1998) was an urban youth development Volunteer in Guyana. She received a B.A. in psychology from Wesleyan University.*

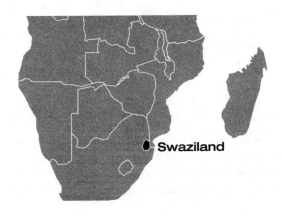

Swaziland

Wood-looking

by Sam Birchall

It was 4:30 a.m. and I was sitting at the "bus station," which is, in fact, a large boulder at the side of the dirt road about a five-minute walk from my house. The moon was bright enough for me to write in my notebook, and the sun was still an hour from rising. I knew that I was at the correct boulder because it was the one that says "Jesus Is Coming" on the side. When I first saw the message glowing dimly in the moonlight, I wondered if He would get here before the bus, and if so, how much He would charge for a lift to Manzini. There was not a soul in sight, and only the crowing of a rooster drowned out the whispers of the wind in a lone pine tree across the road. The boulder was uncomfortable to sit on while trying to write. I could see about a mile down the road, where the bus would be coming from.

Suddenly, I heard voices nearby and then, faintly, the growling sound of the bus, grinding through the gears as it labored up the hill just out of sight. I saw its two glowing eyes as it crested the hill. About fifteen people arrived to board it. I could see the cloud of dust following the bus in the moonlight, looking like a long, sinuous snake.

The ride into town was strenuous and dusty. Whenever the bus stopped, the dust caught up and whooshed in the open windows. Someone had tied a goat on top, and it bleated constantly. The large lady sitting next to me was clutching a chicken in a plastic grocery bag with its head sticking out. Every once in a while it would cluck loudly and struggle to escape the bag, flapping and squawking for a minute before it settled down. The woman paid no attention to it.

In Mbabane, I got my pay—the modest living allowance that all Peace Corps Volunteers receive—did some quick shopping, and arrived at the Peace Corps office at about 9:45 a.m. The transport driver was waiting. It was Bongmusa, the same man who had taken me out to my school when I first arrived in Swaziland. We loaded up and drove to Piggs Peak and on to Mondi Timber. I had written to the manager of Mondi Timber explaining that it was difficult to teach woodworking without wood and asking if he could donate some scraps.

The drive from Mbabane to Piggs Peak was about sixty kilometers. It was a beautifully scenic route. I had started the day at sea level, in a scrub desert climate, and traveled through the middle veld, where the fruit trees and major grain crops were grown, and three hours later I was at 3,500 feet above sea level, driving through towering eucalyptus and pine forests. It was much cooler in the mountains, and the streams were clear, fast, tumbling water, instead of the muddy and sluggish trickles that I was used to.

Mondi Timber was a huge lumber operation with a large sawmill. I found the yard manager and followed him to his office. I introduced myself and explained what I needed. He took me back to the yard and pointed out some piles of rough-sawed, slightly weather-beaten planks, and told me to take what I wanted. I thanked him warmly.

I got the driver to bring the truck around, and we started loading the planks, stacking them neatly in the bed. When the load reached the level of the sides, I was ready to call a halt. Bongmusa disagreed. He explained that since the Peace Corps would let me have the truck only once during the school year, I should get as much lumber as I could. We went back to stacking wood. Bongmusa poked some one-by-twelve planks into the sides, standing on end, and before long, the wood was about a foot higher than the cab. The truck was squatting down in back from the weight of the wood. Finally, Bongmusa was satisfied. We tied the load down as securely as we could. I have never seen a truck so overloaded. I asked Bongmusa if he was sure that we would make it all the way to Elulakeni without breaking down. He assured me that he had carried heavier loads.

As we rolled slowly out the gate of the lumberyard, I felt like Jed Clampett of the *Beverly Hillbillies*. So strong was the feeling that I broke into the theme song. "Well, let me tell y'all a story 'bout a man named Jed, a poor mountaineer, barely kep' his fam'ly fed . . . ."

Bongmusa listened carefully. When I finished, he asked, "Is that a traditional song in America, Sam?"

"Yes, Bongmusa, it is a song that we sing when we have a load that is very large on our trucks," I replied. How else was I going to explain it?

"Was the man named Jed your king? And do your mountains have ears?" He was seriously trying to make sense of the song.

I spent a half-hour trying to explain the premise of the *Beverly Hillbillies* show. It didn't translate that well between our cultures.

Only the first hundred or so miles back to school were on a paved road. As soon as we hit dirt road some of the wood slid off the truck. We stopped and reloaded it and retied it. We did this six times before we reached the school. The rough road made the overloaded truck seem to waddle like a duck. More than once, I thought that we would tip over completely. There was no electricity at Elulakeni, so we unloaded the lumber in darkness, throwing it through the open back door of my woodworking shop, into a huge jumble.

I was extremely happy to have it. There was more than enough wood for all my classes for the next year or more. Some of the wood was going to make benches for my classroom so the boys would have the luxury of sitting.

What a useful thing wood is for a woodworking class. But so far I only had the means to teach "wood-looking." Now all I needed was some tools.

Sam Birchall *(Swaziland 1991-1993) was a woodworking and technical drawing teacher in Elulakeni, in the kingdom of Swaziland. He has a B.A. in economics and management from Wilmington College, Ohio, and lives now in Austin, Texas.*

Fiji

Living by the Book

by Donna Gessell

On Fiji, books were scarce in our village, Naqelewai. All material possessions were scarce because of the village's remote location. Despite the two-day journey involving dusty bus rides and a muddy Land Rover trek, I brought in five cartons of books, many of them Peace Corps issues with titles like *Small Business Projects for Rural Villages* and *Raising Chickens in the Bush.* I also tucked in books for comfort like *The Joy of Cooking, Tao Te Ching,* and *War and Peace.* Later I picked up junk, mystery, and romance novels from other Peace Corps Volunteers and from bookstores in the capital. During my two years in Naqelewai, I read everything I could find, including *Newsweek,* furnished by the Peace Corps, and *National Geographic,* sent by my parents. *National Geographic* may seem a strange choice, given my exotic surroundings, but reading it and piling past issues beside my bed reminded me of my childhood and home.

Reading, however, is not part of the Fijian culture, historically or currently. Before Europeans arrived in the last century, Fijian was not a written language. Early missionaries soon developed English-Fijian dictionaries and translated the Bible into Fijian, so that now almost every rural Fijian home has a copy of the Bible as well as a Fijian hymnal. Few other books find space in the clutter-free house. Newspapers brought in by travelers are read and passed on, then used for a variety of nonliterary purposes, including stencil designs for decoration under the tin cans that hold houseplants, and as crumpled balls used in place of tissue in outdoor toilets. Few rural Fijians read for pleasure, other than the occasional letter from family, although elementary education is almost universal.

Pleasure reading is made difficult because of the lack of electricity. With little artificial light, people in Naqelewai get up with the sun and do most of their activities during daylight. After dark, dinner is served by the light of kerosene lanterns. Conversation follows, sometimes late into the evening, lit by that same dim light.

Despite my investment in a propane lantern, the inevitable eyestrain cut short my periods of night reading. I sometimes read during the after-lunch rest, but reading at other times of the day, when everyone else was working, put me at risk of being thought strange. Wanting to fit in, I tried to limit my appetite for the written word to leisure time.

Sundays, always a favorite day for me to relax with a good book, were not conducive to reading. The day was dedicated to visiting—that is, sitting around and talking for what seemed interminable hours until I finally learned to discuss issues, gossip, and tell jokes in Fijian. During those visits, I learned invaluable information about village life that aided my work, but I often found myself longing to be tucked away with a book.

I enjoyed the intimacy of community discussion, but I missed the intimacy of reading and identifying with fictional characters. My longing made me question my basic assumptions. Which was healthier: participating in community talk or solitary reading?

At times my solitary reading habits became occasion for community talk: "There's Daiana. She always has a book in her hand." In fact, one afternoon when my next-door neighbor came by and found me reading, she voiced her curiosity. She asked if all Americans read as much as I did, if Americans ever neglected their household and family duties to read, and if Americans ever missed work to read a good book. Her questions reminded me of the list of questions posed to suspected alcoholics.

Indeed, other incidents reaffirmed my suspicions that I was a book junkie. One day as I was preparing dinner, a friend came by with out-of-town relatives. After the usual introductions ("Here's our Peace Corps—Daiana"), the woman ventured to demonstrate just how exotic a specimen a "Peace Corps" was. "Look at her," she said, pointing out the cookbook lying open at my side. "She does everything by a book. She even uses one to cook."

Indeed, I began to realize just how much I did "by the book," or "books," to be more precise. For instance, if I wanted to work with the village nurse on a nutrition education project, I consulted the *Lik-Lik Book* for information about projects conducted by village development workers in Papua New Guinea. I looked up food information and recipes in the Fijian Women's Club *Kakana Vinaka* and Susan Parker's *Fijian Cookbook*. I consulted food leaflets my Peace Corps Volunteer friend Sikandra Spain was developing for the South Pacific Commission. I used Peace Corps manuals to get ideas for poster presentations. And it wasn't just Peace Corps projects that sent me to books. I read for pleasure, falling asleep and waking up with books.

It is no wonder that when my house accidentally caught fire, the first items the Fijians rushed to save were the books. They knew what was important to me. Despite the almost irreplaceable pieces of Fijian tapa cloth and a war club hanging in the house, they reached for my books first. They recognized my values even though they did not share them.

It is not surprising that of all my projects in Naqelewai, the primary school library is my lasting legacy. When the school was being rebuilt, the headmaster requested a library. He set aside the space in the building, and I contacted agencies that collect and distribute new and used books. Ten chests of books arrived, and some fifth and sixth graders helped sort and process the books. When the new building was finished, the headmaster declared the library the most important part of the new school, and he predicted a long future of reading for his students.

Donna Gessell *(Fiji 1979-1982) was a community development Volunteer in Naqelewai, Fiji, where she worked with five villages on development projects, and in Suva, Fiji, where she helped train women community leaders from across the Pacific at the Community Education Training Center of the South Pacific Commission. Gessell has a doctorate in English literature from Case Western Reserve University and is assistant professor of English at North Georgia State University.*

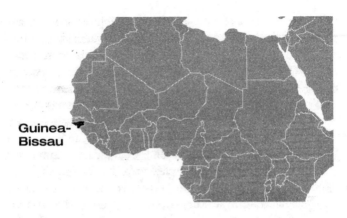

Guinea-Bissau

My Side vs. Their Side

by Roz Wollmering

My Side

I entered the school brimming with ideas, innovative teaching methods, and the desire to have an effect. It was the first day of school in Guinea-Bissau, the tiny West African country where I had been assigned as an English teacher with the Peace Corps. After completing an exhausting and demanding twelve weeks of training in language as well as cross-cultural and technical skills, I felt more than adequately prepared for the challenge of teaching in a poor school system designed on a colonial model.

Inside the building, I noticed a strange absence of noise. A few students wearing white school jackets rambled about in the dimly lit hallway. As I neared the stairs to the administrative office, I heard a mango drop to the ground outside and a sudden chorus of children's voices. Hoping to catch a glimpse of the fastest one carrying off the ripe prize, I looked out into the schoolyard and saw instead piles of old desks, broken bricks, and tree branches. They must be cleaning the school grounds, I thought to myself. When I entered the office, the principal and his assistant were looking at a class schedule posted on the wall and discussing the large number of teachers who still needed to be hired by the Ministry. After greeting me warmly by inquiring about my health, my family back in America, and my life in general, they informed me that my teaching load had been increased by eight hours since the previous week. "No problem," I responded, "I love to teach."

I glanced at my watch, excused myself, and hurried to my first class, which was located a short distance behind the main building. Three lines of classrooms were arranged in rows, like military barracks. Since it was the first day of classes, I hopped on my bicycle and coasted right up to the door of classroom number nineteen—my classroom. "Always wiser to be punctual and prepared than tardy and unequipped," I told myself. Two students were sitting inside the classroom, playing cards, when I entered. I looked at the official enrollment number of forty-seven and asked earnestly, "Where are the other students?" The card players faltered a bit and then mumbled, "They'll come, by and by."

"Well, let's begin without them," I suggested, with a disapproving stare at the cards. They shrugged their shoulders and offered to go and find the students. It certainly didn't seem reasonable to me to teach two students and then have to teach the same material again when the others showed up. Be flexible, I reminded myself, and so I agreed.

One week later, there were twenty-six students outside my classroom, waiting for the rest of their classmates to appear "by and by." They refused to enter until all the enrolled students had showed up. I noticed that not only were students absent, but teachers as well. Meanwhile, the principal and his assistant were still discussing the schedule on the wall, moving multicolored pins, and deliberating about how best to resolve the shortage of teachers. That morning I had stopped by the administrative office again just to make sure that I had understood correctly the radio announcement made by the minister of education the previous evening. I thought that he had announced that classes were in session and was quite relieved when the principal verified my assessment. He then asked me to teach an additional two hours a week. Lacking the experience to rebut his statement that "when there's a lack of teachers, we all need to pitch in a few extra hours," I nodded in consent. Considering that I wasn't actually teaching any students at the time, two extra hours didn't seem much of a burden, and I left, feeling only a mild premonition that I might regret it later.

By the end of the third week, I had managed to convince, cajole, and beg my students to enter the classroom. What other teachers did was their decision, I figured, but as for me, I was itching to do something other than wait on shore like a seafarer's wife. Once the students had entered, I discovered to my amazement that I couldn't get them to quiet down. Ignoring my requests to pay attention, they continued to socialize. Daisy painted her nails and chatted with Aminata about the new discotheque called Temptation that had just opened across from the mosque. Bebe took Nanda's notebook and wouldn't return it. Fatu gave me the peace sign and went outside to urinate. A few others followed. Students wandered in late with irrelevant excuses like "It's hot" or "I'm tired." Nelson and Marcelino held competitive "jive" talks while their classmates gathered around encouraging first one and then the other. Other students, whose teachers were absent, hung around the open windows, throwing crumpled-up balls of paper to their friends. Others simply came to stare at me, a white woman who rode a bicycle to school. They shoved up against the outside wall, clambered over each other's backs, and stuck their heads in for a peek, yelling, "White woman, white woman, there she is!" The next day, still more "window students" appeared to torment me. Such behavior continued daily. Eventually I began to yell at them—"Get away from the windows!"—and resorted to pushing them out of viewing range. After a month at my new post, I reigned over thirty hours a week of complete disorder in a pseudo-classroom kingdom. This is madness, I thought.

For the next month, I devoted the first twenty minutes of class solely to establishing peace and quiet. I was determined. I did this with gentle coaxes at first, but gradually evolved to using threats ("I'll call the school disciplinarian!") and offering sweet enticement ("If you're good, I'll let you out early!"). Late students were not allowed to enter, regardless of their excuses. It seemed the only way to control the chaos. Once I had my students' attention, I made them copy page after page of notes from the blackboard into their notebooks. I wanted to inundate their minds with grammar rules and vocabulary lists so they wouldn't have time to talk. Other times, I made them repeat sentences in unison as if they were Berlitz parrots. Audio-lingual theorists suggest that language is acquired through repetition of recurring patterns, a proposition effectively demonstrated when I overheard my students mimicking me: "Be quiet! Go sit down!"

When the drudgery of memorization and repetition began to bore even me, I resorted to playing bingo, Simon Says, or Do the Hokey-Pokey. I went to elaborate lengths to make nifty prizes for positive reinforcement and spent countless hours designing educational posters for the walls. For a time, I concentrated on visual stimulation and drama to reinforce right-brain learning, but the posters disappeared overnight and the drama idea erupted one day during a production of a local folk tale: My fellow teachers disapproved of thrashing crocodiles, bellowing hippos, and trumpeting elephants during school hours. The students whined like eight-year-olds and threw verbal tantrums when they could no longer perform or play games. I rather enjoyed their drama productions myself, and I figured they were reviewing English grammar and vocabulary by playing the games. But deep inside of me arose a persistent, nagging voice: "Surely you can do more than baby-sit."

Gradually, as discipline turned my classroom into a virtual boot camp, my classes began to develop a catatonic personality. Somber students stared back at me or out into space. Apathy replaced the boisterous noise I had grown accustomed to fighting. They refused to open their notebooks until I'd repeated the request three times. Orders and instructions mollified them, sure enough, but now they didn't seem to have opinions, concerns, or even interests. Some simply put their heads down and slept. Sit and listen they did, but participate and discuss and collaborate they did not. Their passive resistance soon infuriated me, and I yelled in frustration at them, "I am here to help you. Don't you understand that?" They stared at me in dazed disbelief. "What do you want?" I implored them with open hands: "Do you want me to entertain you? To treat you like military recruits? To punish you?" They shrugged their shoulders and sighed, "Teacher, we are pitiful. That's life." "Go," I told them. "Go home. Get out." They refused, of course.

Against my better judgment, I finally called in the school disciplinarian. The moment he arrived, every single student in the classroom jumped up to attention. They greeted him in perfect unison with a resounding "Good morning, Mr. Disciplinarian." When he ordered them to sit down, an immaculate silence spread throughout the classroom. I was astounded. They looked so serene and innocent as they waited attentively for his words. Their perfect composure made them look like harmless babes, and I began to imagine that they would convince him of their purity and that I was the evil abuser. I began to wonder, in fact, if this wasn't perhaps partially true.

The disciplinarian picked out several students who were not wearing school jackets, and a few who were but had not buttoned the top button. He accused them of intentionally belittling their American teacher and expelled them for two weeks. He then read a list of seven students' names. Since these students had registered for classes but had not yet paid their school fees, he expelled them for the year, adding an insult as they crept out of the classroom. He then turned to me and said, "If any of these students ever give you a problem, no matter how small, you tell me, and I will expel the entire class for the entire year. Not one of them will pass, and they will all have to repeat the year." As I struggled to come up with a suitable response, he turned back to the students, held up one finger, and challenged them, "Just one of you try it. Just one, and I'll whip your ass." And then he left. I stood in horrified shock and embarrassment. I had just lost thirteen students. The students said nothing. They stared at me and waited to see what I would do next. I felt angry and stupid and offered a feeble apology. I fumed all the way home.

That night I dreaded going back to the classroom the next morning. I thought about ending my Peace Corps service and going home. I was sure I could find a justifiable excuse for a graceful exit. It was now the third month of teaching and quarterly grades were due in ten days. All I had managed to teach were two review units. Two review units! Most of these students couldn't even meet the standards of the previous year's curriculum! How did they manage to pass? I was tempted to flunk them all myself this time around, but what would that accomplish? I looked in dismay at the stack of twenty-five lesson plans I had diligently prepared during the late-night hours of the past two months and realized that I would never use them.

So I switched strategies. That night I drew up a "No More" list. No more colorful visual aids to catch their attention. No more fancy vocabulary and grammar handouts. No more games. No more prizes. And no more school disciplinarian to resolve crises.

My next unit began with the following dialogue:

Teacher:	I am angry. I cannot teach because you do not respect me.
Students:	No, no, Teacher. Please, Teacher, please.
Teacher:	I don't want to teach you. I'm leaving.
Students:	No, Teacher, no. Please, Teacher. You see, you don't understand our situation.
Teacher:	Well, tell me, just what is your "situation"?

This time the dialogue was theirs to complete and resolve.

Their Side

It was Tino and Mando who came and told us that a skinny, white woman had jumped off a bicycle, run into our classroom, and tried to teach them English that morning. Tino and Mando weren't even in our class. They were just sitting there waiting to use the soccer field when she rushed in like the rains. They weren't sure what to say because she looked so strange. Her hair was all falling down, and she wore a dress that looked like an old faded bed covering that one might have bought from a Mauritanian vendor in the used-clothing market. We all walked over to Nito's house and found a few more of our classmates sitting out back drinking frothy tea. We decided, even though school hadn't really started yet, that we'd go the next day to see what this new American teacher looked like. Tino and Mando assured us that she was as ugly as a newly hatched, greedy-eyed vulture.

We knew that almost no one would be at school yet. Most students were still on the farms, finishing the harvest, and others were still trying to register and pay their fees. The Ministry had changed the admission rules again. All registrations completed at the end of the last year were now declared invalid, and so we had to wait in line, get new photographs, show our papers, and pay fees all over again—either that or pay some official to put our names on the list, which actually was much easier than completing the registration process. We listened to the radio broadcasts of the minister, reminding parents about the importance of school. Everybody knew he sent his children to the private Portuguese school.

As it turned out, we agreed to enter the classroom just when everyone else did. We always say: "Cross the river in a crowd and the crocodile won't eat you." From that first day, she never demanded our respect. She didn't seem to care if we wore our school jackets or not. She didn't write the teaching summary on the board like our other teachers, and she was always in the classroom before the bell rang. That meant we could never stand up and honor her entrance. She should have known not to enter until after the bell rang. And she never took roll call first, as she should have, and so we continued talking and doing our homework. Of course, by this time, other students had heard about our white woman teacher and were coming by to look at her and watch our class. We couldn't resist joining in the fun. At times, we believed she was serious, for example, when she told the students outside class to leave. But where were they supposed to go? The area in front of her classroom was the designated student recreation area. Instead of ignoring them and us, she berated them with gestures and scolded us in Portuguese. Her Portuguese wasn't bad, but it sounded so funny when she said "Spoiled brats!" that you just had to laugh. We laughed even harder every time she said "Peace Corps" because in our Kriolu language, "Peace Corps" sounds like "body of fish." We called her the "fish-body teacher" after that.

Classes were interesting because they were unpredictable. She kept switching her methods, and we were never sure what to expect next. For a while she insisted that the mind equips itself and a teacher must not interfere in the process. She called that "the silent way." After "the silent way" came "total physical response." We gave actions to everything and pretended to be desks, pencils, and other classroom articles. We twisted our bodies around and played What Am I? Then we role-played imaginary dialogues between, for example, two books fighting to get into a book bag at the same time. One day she taught us the song "In the Jungle." We loved that song. No, you couldn't really call her a consistent person, but we all have our little ways. Even so, "a cracked calabash can still be mended." Obviously, she cared about us because she worked so hard to prepare for class. Most of our teachers were so busy at home or working a second or third job that they often missed class, and when they did show up, they had never prepared anything. It's true that we've already learned more English this quarter than we learned all last year.

We always wanted to do more activities and play new games, but she thought we needed to write. Because we didn't have books, she kept demanding that we copy information down on paper. But Guineans are oral people. We learn by talking; we make discoveries by sharing our experiences; and we help others by listening and contributing to conversations. Our history is a collective memory, and we are continually passing our knowledge on to others in our speech. She wanted us to raise our hands, one by one, and then talk individually. To us that seemed wrong.

She confused us even more by saying pointless things with vigor—"Wake up! Discover yourselves!"—or asking questions that had no obvious answers: "Why are you here?" or "What are you going to do?" Then she'd wait with such an intent expression on her face that we'd say almost anything to try to please her. We always enjoyed her facial expressions because they foretold what was to follow—anger, joy, disappointment, praise, or contentment. She really should have learned by then how to hide or show her feelings to suit her purpose more effectively, but she didn't seem to care. In some ways, she was just like a child.

We just didn't understand why it was our thinking that needed to change, and never hers. She wore a "bad eye" charm around her neck, so we thought she was superstitious, but when we asked her, she said she wore it to show respect for our culture. We asked her if that was why foreigners always wanted to buy our ritual masks and initiation staffs, but she didn't answer. She told us we didn't need World Bank handouts and International Monetary Fund debts. What we needed, she said, was to learn how to raise fish. Was she crazy? We need computers, not fish! Balanta women always know where to find fish. "Teacher," we told her, "you will come and go, but we stay here." How could she understand our culture? She had only seen the rains fall once.

After a while, the novelty wore off, and we got tired of even a white woman's ways. It's hard—waking up at daybreak, doing morning chores, and then going to school for five hours without eating breakfast. Her class was during the last hour, and we were as hungry as wild animals by that time. Some of us lived far from school, and if our step-uncle or older cousin-brother told us to go to the market before school, we had no choice. We were forced to run to her class with only a bellyful of worms because we knew she wouldn't listen to our misfortunes even if we arrived two minutes late. It's true! In America, time is money, but here time is different. Time is just now, nothing more.

It wasn't only that we had responsibilities at home that came before school—sometimes we were sick. If we had malaria, we'd put our heads down and sleep. And if we had "runny belly," we'd just run out of class when the cramping started. The dry season was so hot that we faded away like the songs of morning birds. One day she yelled at us. We admit we weren't cooperating, but people are like that. We forgive each other and just go on. "That's life," we'd tell her. "A log, as long as it stays in the water, will never become a crocodile." Many things we just accepted as natural, but she considered such an attitude "fatalistic."

Finally, she called the school disciplinarian on us. She should have done that much earlier, in our opinion. We played our roles by allowing him to throw out a few students because we all knew they'd be back as soon as he got some cashew-wine money from them. Anyway, that's the right of elders in our culture, and we're taught in the bush to live by the established rules. We didn't understand why she apologized after he left, and we couldn't believe it when she undermined his authority by apologizing for his "poisonous pedagogy," as she called it. Like a Guinean woman, she certainly had courage.

Today, she did something different again. She came in and wrote a dialogue on the board. She asked questions about the dialogue that made us disagree. We had a lively discussion in English and then got into our groups and began designing some solutions for the problem presented in the dialogue. We always say, "When the ants unite their mouths, they can carry an elephant."

We know she'll stay, too. We saw it in her eyes.

Roz Wollmering *(Guinea-Bissau 1990-1992) has an M.A. in Chinese from the University of Minnesota and a B.A. in Spanish and biology from St. Cloud State University, Minnesota. She is a former associate Peace Corps director in the Baltics.*

Mongolia

Cold Mornings

by Matthew Heller

Our family always lived where we needed a snow shovel. I remember one snowstorm in particular when I was nine. My best friend, Bobby Frost, and I shoveled my entire driveway ourselves, which is no small feat for nine-year-olds. When we were done, my father was waiting in the kitchen to reward us with grilled cheese sandwiches, tomato soup, and a silver dollar for the work we had done. Dipping my grilled cheese into the steaming tomato soup (in my opinion, truly the best way to eat the two together), I am sure I was oblivious to how lucky I was, to how Norman Rockwell-beautiful shoveling a driveway can be.

Because I grew up in New England, winter was always my favorite season. It meant ice hockey, snow days off from school, and sledding until dinner was ready. Winter meant scratchy wool hats, scarves that always choked me, jackets that made me look like a mini-sumo wrestler, snow pants that made peeing an ordeal, and moon boots. My moon boots were my favorite. I may even have worn them to bed a few times, afraid someone would take them from me while I slept. I loved winter as much as I loved those moon boots.

I still love winter, but to say I enjoy it as I did when I was nine years old would be a lie. I've been a Peace Corps Volunteer in Mongolia for eighteen months now and I live in a *ger*, a tent with a small wood stove in the center. It is strong and practical, the perfect domicile for a nomadic herder living on the Asian steppe. It packs up in about half an hour. I, however, am not a herder, but an English teacher in a small secondary school in rural Mongolia. *Ger* life is not easy. It makes twenty-year-olds look thirty-five. It makes your soul hard.

Mongolians are very proud of their history and traditions. Once, while I was sitting on the train going from Ulaanbaatar, the capital of Mongolia, to my own town, Bor-Undur, a Mongolian pointed to his arm and said, "In here is the blood of Genghis Khan. Beware." Really, there is no argument to that statement. I responded, "Yes, older brother (a respectful title addressed to elders), your country is beautiful. Mongolians are lucky people."

Unfortunately, many Mongolians are big vodka drinkers, and this very drunk herder was on his way home from selling cashmere wool and meat in the city. He had been successful in his business, was celebrating, and wanted to teach me the custom of taking the traditional three shots of vodka that new acquaintances must drink. His shots were too big for me, and I only wanted to taste the vodka, not help him finish the bottle. That's when Genghis' blood came into the conversation. I drank the three shots. Herders are tough people. They don't wear moon boots.

Maybe if I had been born here and lived in a *ger* all my life, I would be tough, too. But I wasn't, and I'm not. I can trace no lineage to the man who was once the world's most powerful ruler, but I am blessed. I am blessed with the gift of a Peace Corps/Mongolia standard-issue sleeping bag rated to -30 degrees. When combined with another sleeping bag of my own and some wool blankets, I am completely protected from the cold that invades my *ger* every night when the fire goes out.

When it's time to wake up and start my day, the first thing I do is build a fire. In the quiet darkness of morning, huddling next to my stove and sipping hot coffee, I listen to the Voice of America on my shortwave radio and remind myself who I am, where I'm from, and what I'm doing. I'm a young Volunteer spending eight hours a day with Mongolians, building a greenhouse with the other teachers in my school so there will be more vegetables in our town. Along with many other things, I'm learning how they live. In the steppe there is very little snow, only biting wind and dust. It gets as cold as -50 degrees, not counting the wind chill factor. If I leave leftover tea in a mug, it will freeze solid by morning. I've broken three mugs that way. When it is this cold I sometimes ask myself, "How valuable is the contribution I'm making? And is it really worth being this cold?"

For eighteen months now I've been waking up and thinking, yes, it is. I love working with Mongolians, but the time of day I look forward to most is building my morning fire. It is my time of epiphany. As I feel the warmth that my own hands created, a fire that pushes back the cold and the dark, replacing them with warmth and light, I know I will live another day. Such an experience defines what it means to be a Peace Corps Volunteer.

We all build fires in one way or other, and the warmth we create is as good as eating grilled cheese sandwiches and tomato soup on a winter day when you're only nine years old. Being a Volunteer in Mongolia and having the opportunity to live in a *ger* may mean enduring very cold mornings, but it's worth more than all the silver dollars in the world.

Matthew Heller *(Mongolia 1995-1997) was an English teacher in Bor-Undur, Mongolia, where he taught secondary school students and facilitated a greenhouse reconstruction project. Heller has a B.A. in English from Whitman College in Walla Walla, Washington.*

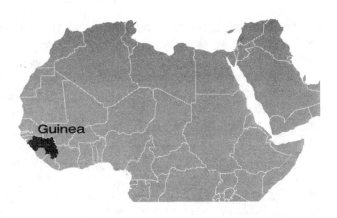

Shades of Gray

by Josh Johnson

When I lived in Guinea, in West Africa, I answered to many names. My passport said I was Josh. I was also Georges and Jacques—francophone interpretations of "Josh" in the mouths of my local colleagues. Certain students called me "Klinsmann," after a German soccer star whose hair was said to resemble mine. After a while, I became Fode Moussa—"learned Moses"—to friends who decided I should have an African name.

And all children under a certain age had their own name for me: *foté*, or "white person" in the Susu language.

Peace Corps literature is comprehensive on the subject of local names for outsiders. In West Africa alone, an American can be called *foté, toubab, porto, kweepolo, yovo,* and dozens of other names in other languages. Etymologies are inconsistent. *Toubab* means doctor in Wolof. The Fula *porto* is thought to be derived from the word "Portuguese," after the first European explorers.

74

Foté literally refers to the color white, though the usage is flexible. An African-American Volunteer who lived in a village near me was called *foté-noir*—the black white man.

All of this name-calling seemed rude. I tried to explain this. No, people assured me, the word *foté* was intended neither as insult nor as mockery. It was a friendly greeting, they said, for people who did not know my name. But I noticed that older, more educated people tended not to use the word. Never was it spoken by anyone who seemed interested in being my friend, except for children, who wielded it without mercy.

I noticed that local women, when they saw me coming, would often begin whispering to their young children. Invariably, the child's eyes would widen in terror and the child would begin to shriek, pressing his or her face into the folds of the mother's clothing.

Unnerved by this, I once asked a bystander for an explanation. He laughed. "Mothers like to scare their children by telling them, 'There's the *foté*! He's coming to take you away!'"

I protested that this was cruel, and that it made things difficult for me. My protest was in vain. I had come thousands of miles to live in a place I didn't understand, with people whose language continued to escape me. And now, a white man in a black country, I was the bogeyman.

Once these cowering toddlers got a little older, they seemed to lose their fear of me. It was as if, in groups, they felt emboldened to confront the bogeyman. They evidently believed that if they screamed my name loudly enough, they could overcome my power to spirit them away. They would call out as I passed: first a lone voice, then a chorus. These older children now clung to each other rather than their mothers; it was their job to keep up the chant, warding me off. *"FOTÉ! FOTÉ! FOTÉ!"*

Early one morning during the first week at my town in Guinea, I was riding my bicycle to the school where I taught English. My feet were heavy on the pedals. I was lonely and depressed, overwhelmed by the newness of everything. Everyone who knew me well was 5,000 miles away. The road passed through three miles of trees and rice fields. The sun appeared over the mountains behind me. I came to a point where the trees on either side of the road grew together, forming a canopy, a marvelous shady amphitheater that each morning was alive with birdsong.

I slowed and concentrated on the birds. My spirits began to rise. At times like this—the birds, the mountains, the early morning light on the unbelievable green of the rice paddies—I couldn't imagine living in a more beautiful place. Then—I hadn't even noticed the young boy at the side of the road—it began. *"Foté!"* A half-dozen children appeared, shattering the morning's peace. *"FOTÉ! FOTÉ! FOTÉ! FOTÉ! FOTÉ! FOTÉ!"*

It might seem incredible to anyone who hasn't been in a similar situation, the power of these small children over my mood. My self-consciousness returned, that awful feeling I was having far too often of being uncomfortable in my own skin. I thought: I don't belong here.

Then, up ahead, a Guinean man emerged from a roadside cafe and began sweeping its concrete veranda. At the moment I noticed him, he happened to look up and see me, moving slowly up the hill. The screaming kids were keeping pace with my bicycle. My sense of shame deepened. It was worse to have a witness. How could I be a serious person and let myself be tormented like this by eight-year-olds? But the man surprised me. In a friendly, confident voice, he called out the first English greeting I had heard in a week: "Hello, my black brother! How's the day?"

Had he watched the scene, understood my desperation? Was this irony? He seemed in earnest. He waved. A wide smile crossed his face, as though to broadcast satisfaction at having successfully wrestled with the dim memory of an English lesson. Whatever his motivation, it didn't matter. The spell was broken. The words of the children suddenly seemed small and unimportant. As I picked up speed I answered, "Good morning, my brother." I offered no correction to his adjective. Though I was an English teacher, this was a misuse of the language I could live with.

Josh Johnson *(Guinea 1996-1999) was an English teacher in Dubreka, Guinea, for two years. He was a regional representative in Kankan, Guinea, for his third year of service. Johnson has a B.S. in journalism from the University of Colorado at Boulder and a master's degree from the Columbia University School of Journalism.*

To Peel Potatoes

by John P. Deever

"Life's too short to peel potatoes," a woman in my local supermarket announced, as she put a box of instant mashed potatoes into her cart. When I overheard her I nearly exploded.

After recently returning from my Peace Corps stint in Ukraine, I tend to get defensive about the potato in all its forms: sliced, scalloped, diced, chopped, grated, or julienned; then boiled, browned, french-fried, slow-fried, mashed, baked, or twice-baked—with a dollop of butter or sour cream, yes, thank you.

A large proportion of my time in Ukraine was spent preparing what was, in the winter, nearly the only vegetable available. Minutes and hours added up to days spent handling potatoes. I sized up the biggest, healthiest spuds in the market and bought bucketfuls, then hauled them home over icy sidewalks.

Winter evenings, when it got dark at four p.m., I scrubbed my potatoes thoroughly under the icy tap—we had no hot water—until my hands were numb. Though I like the rough, sour peel and prefer potatoes skin-on, Chernobyl radiation lingered in the local soil, so we were advised to strip off the skins. I peeled and peeled, pulling the dull knife toward my thumb as Svetlana Adamovna had taught me, and brown-flecked stripe after stripe dropped off to reveal a golden tuber beneath. Finally, I sliced them into boiling water or a hot frying pan. My potatoes, my *kartopli*, sizzled and cooked through, warming up my tiny kitchen in the dormitory until the windows clouded over with steam.

Very often my Ukrainian friends and I peeled and cooked potatoes together, either in my kitchen or in Tanya's or Misha's or Luda's, all the while laughing and talking and learning from each other. Preparing potatoes became for me both a happy prelude to nourishment and, when shared with others, an interactive ritual giving wider scope and breadth to my life.

But how could I explain that feeling to the Instant Woman in a grocery store in the United States? I wanted to say, "On the contrary, life's too short for instant anything."

Now, back home, I'm pressed by all the "instant" things to do. In Ukraine, accomplishing two simple objectives in one day—like successfully phoning Kiev from the post office and then finding a store with milk—satisfied me pretty well. I taught my classes, worked on other projects, and tried to stay happy and healthy along the way.

Now it takes an hour of fast driving to get to work, as opposed to twelve minutes of leisurely walking in Ukraine. I spend hours fiddling with my computer to send "instant" e-mail. Talking to three people at once during a phone call is efficient—not an accident of Soviet technology as in Ukraine. With so much time-saving, I ought to have hours and hours to peel potatoes. Somehow I don't.

What I wish I'd said to the woman in the supermarket is this: "Life's too short to be shortened by speeding it up."

But I wasn't able to formulate that thought so quickly. Instead, I went to the frozen food section and stared at the microwave dinners for a while, eventually coming to the sad, heavy realization that the Szechuan chicken looked delicious—even if it didn't come with potatoes.

John P. Deever *(Ukraine 1993-1995) works at the Haas School of Business at the University of California, Berkeley. This essay won the 1996 Peace Corps Experience Award given by RPCV Writers & Readers.*

Tonga

Under the Tongan Sun
by Tina Martin

On Tonga, I lived in a tiny hut made of bamboo and coconut leaves and lined with dozens of mats, pieces of tapa cloth, and wall-to-wall children. When I sat on the floor with my back against the rear door, my feet almost touched the front door. There was no electricity or running water, so I used a kerosene lamp and drew water from the well. There were breadfruit trees and avocado trees around my hut, and if I wanted a coconut, the children climbed a tree for me.

The kids I taught were always with me, and I loved them even more than I once loved my privacy. I always wanted to have children, but I never thought I'd have so many and have them so soon. These were the children I would like to have around me back home—children who had never seen a television set and didn't depend upon "things" for their entertainment because they didn't have any "things." For fun, they taught each other dances and songs, and they juggled oranges.

They woke me up each morning, calling through my bamboo poles. They took my five seniti and got me freshly baked bread from the shop across the lawn, and they helped me eat it. Some of them watched the ritual of my morning bath—water drawn from the well and heated on my kerosene stove and poured into a tin, then over a pre-soaped me. They sometimes braided my hair and helped me get dressed for school. Then they walked me there, where I used the oral English method we learned in training—acting out the language so there's no need for translation.

"I'm running! I'm running!" I said as I ran in front of the class. "I'm running! I'm running!" I took a child by the hand.

"Run!" I said, and eventually he did. The goal was to have a running paradigm, which usually ended, "I running, you running, he/she/it running." We did this for all verbs. English was the link between Tonga and all other land masses of the world. And English was the exercise that kept me scrawny, the worst physical defect a body could have in the Tongan culture, where fat is beautiful. I tried to compensate for my lack of bulk by being very *anga lelei* (good-natured), which was their most cherished personality trait.

After school, the children would come home with me and stay, singing Tongan songs and the songs I'd taught them.

Then I tried to help them prepare for the sixth-grade exam that would determine their scholastic future. And they helped me prepare whichever vegetable was to be my dinner.

The children never left until I was safely tucked into bed under my canopy of mosquito net on top of tapa cloth. Then I blew out my lamp, lay down, and listened to the songs from a kava ceremony nearby. Sometimes there was light from what a Tongan teacher told me was now the American moon, since we had put a man there.

On moonless nights, I fell asleep in complete darkness. But I fell asleep knowing that I would always wake up under the Tongan sun.

Tina Martin *(Tonga 1969-1971) began her career in English as a second language as a teacher-trainer Volunteer in Tonga. After her service in the Peace Corps, she went on to teach in Spain and Algeria. She is now an ESL instructor at City College of San Francisco.*

Morocco

Neighbors

by Orin Hargraves

It was a hot, dusty afternoon in late August. I had just
returned to El Hajeb, the village where I had taught English
for a year. I'd been away for the summer: a few weeks of
being surrounded by Volunteers old and new at that year's
omnibus training program in Rabat, the capital. El Hajeb
was a big comedown after all that. I was the only American
in town, and though I'd been quite happy with that for a
year, coming back to it all at once was a shock. I hadn't yet
rediscovered any of the parts about it that I liked.

I spent most of the afternoon writing letters, catching
up on correspondence that had piled up in my mailbox
while I was away. I was also conveniently avoiding the
heat, and, to some degree, the village itself. At that
moment it didn't feel like the place I wanted to be. I stayed
inside the thick, cool, stuccoed walls of my fine house. You
see, mine wasn't the mud-hut Peace Corps experience. I
lived in the upstairs apartment of a beautiful colonial-peri-

od villa in the part of the town that had been built by the French. Walnut trees lined the avenue outside, and I could hear boys throwing stones up into them, trying to knock down the ripening fruit.

A cool breeze from the mountains picked up late in the afternoon, intimating that it might bring some clouds our way, along with a shower or thunderstorm. I took advantage of the cooler air to get a little exercise and walked to the post office. I felt fortified now after the hours of seclusion, ready to withstand the stares of the children, and the cries of "Christian! Christian!" that often accompanied me on my walks in the village.

The post office offered the usual experience: a cluster of people mashed together in front of the sullen clerk, all thrusting their business in his face, with the line of less determined off to one side, standing patiently in the belief that they would be waited on sometime. I joined the line, not yet feeling up to the cluster experience. It took ten minutes or so, but this way I could stay inside the thick American shell that I still wasn't willing to leave.

When I started back, the rain was looking like a sure thing. The breeze had become a wind. Little dust devils were whirling around in the dirt streets, and withered leaves twirled down from the sycamore trees that formed an arcade over the wide, dilapidated street. Dark clouds were bearing down from the mountains to the south. I picked up my pace, thinking that now I'd have to hurry to get in before the rain.

Down the street, coming toward me, was a woman wrapped in a turquoise *jellaba*. I recognized her as my downstairs neighbor. She wasn't veiled and her hood was off: This was only a walk in the neighborhood and she wouldn't be subject to the prying eyes of students. As we continued toward each other, we were nearly jogging, trying to reach our destinations before the rain. Under these circumstances, the normal greeting rituals—which could run a few minutes of chattering even with someone you saw all the time—would be overlooked. We only exchanged smiles and hello, how-are-yous as we passed.

"Please tell Aisha to put the goats in the shed. It's going to rain," she shouted at me over her shoulder as she continued on her way.

"Okay," I said.

In that moment, such a feeling of elation! And why, over something so small and trivial? Because she said it in Arabic, not in French. Because she didn't slow down or dress it up for speaking to a foreigner. Because she said it to me in the same way she would have said it to one of her own children, or one of her other neighbors: without formality, without any awareness that she was talking to someone from the other side of the world, but just saying it the way she normally would say it. Because after all, I was only her neighbor, no one strange or special. I was just the guy who lived upstairs.

Orin Hargraves *(Morocco 1980-1982) was a TEFL Volunteer in El Hajeb, Morocco, where he taught English in the local high school. Hargraves has a B.A. from the University of Chicago and is the author of* Culture Shock! Morocco: A Guide to Customs and Etiquette.

Dominican Republic

Not Just Any Other Day
by Dianne Garyantes

I walked into the well-lit, freshly painted office building—late, as expected. This was the custom in the Dominican Republic; meetings always started late. As I entered, I wiped the mud from my shoes; it had been raining all day in the little village where I worked. A small knot of women in faded dresses and flip-flops was huddled in the center of a large meeting room. Maybe I had pushed the lateness thing too far, I thought, because they were waiting for me.

I had been asked by the local women's club to speak on a panel for International Women's Day. When I was first approached to speak, I hesitated. This would not be a discussion about AIDS awareness or planning a community project. I would have to say something about life, about women, about who we are and what we could become. During my past year in the village, I had been humbled by the harsh conditions around me and the grace with which people managed to live. Families worked three harvests a year in the nearby rice fields, they nurtured supportive relationships with their families and neighbors, and most kept three or four sources of income flowing into the household. Who was I to speak to them about life or who they were? I decided my talk would have to be a discussion in which the women themselves would rely on their innate wisdom and worth.

It was a surprise to me that the women's club was acknowledging International Women's Day. The women in the club usually came together to be social, to trade sewing tips, to escape from the everyday events of the household. They were not politically active and did not identify themselves as a subordinate or marginalized group because they were women. My guess was that I had been asked to speak that day because I was a somewhat exotic *americana,* not because I was a woman.

My first glance into the meeting room told me my instincts were correct. All of the other panelists for the day were men. Although I knew that in the Dominican Republic men were viewed as the ones who spoke with and for authority, it was still a shock. This was International Women's Day! The day was set aside to celebrate women and our accomplishments. I was filled with a new sense of purpose as I walked to the front of the room.

When it was the *americana's* turn to speak, I asked the women in the audience to list all the essentials of life, things we all need as human beings to survive. I wrote the responses on a poster board as they came at a rapid-fire pace: good health, shelter, food, water, children and family, clothing, medicine, education. The list went on until the poster board was full.

Next, we circled in red the items on the list for which women in the Dominican Republic were responsible. The answers this time came more slowly. The first person to respond said that women in the Dominican Republic were responsible for caring for children and families. Another hand went up to point out that women collect water every day for drinking, cleaning, bathing, and cooking. We realized that women also are responsible for keeping the family healthy and getting medicine when someone is sick. Women also make sure that homework is done and that children are in school every day. Meals, clothing, and cleaning and maintenance of the home are also under the responsibility of women. We continued to circle items on the list until every single suggestion on the poster board was surrounded by red. The air in the room became thick with stunned silence.

I felt exhilarated and a little dazed by the enormity of our conclusion. All the items on the list were the responsibility of the women sitting in the room. Women were making daily decisions and carrying out responsibilities that were nothing less than essential to life. They were essential to life! Our list, cheerful with bright red circles, affirmed this.

As in societies and cultures everywhere, men and women in the Dominican Republic share in the responsibilities for their families, communities, and country. The difference is that women are seldom acknowledged, celebrated, or rewarded for their contributions. The women in the audience felt this lack of appreciation every day as they ate last, after their husbands and children, and rarely, if ever, shared a meal at the same table as their spouses. Instead, they sat in the kitchen at the back of the house, taking quick mouthfuls of food in between serving and cleaning up after the others. Many of the women in the audience also were raising children conceived by their husbands outside their marriage. And many had been put down or ignored all their lives. Who, after all, was the boss? Who, after all, was important?

One of the women in the audience was Gloria, who worked two jobs as a nurse and traveled forty kilometers in the back of a pick up truck for one of her jobs. She also swept and mopped her house each day, raised a young son, and helped cultivate bananas, plantains, and cocoa for additional income. When the community needed help raising money to build a school, Gloria organized collections in the local church and raised more than $300 for the project.

Idaylia, who was also there that day, had a disabled left foot, yet still started each day by collecting water for her family. This meant at least three trips to and from the village's water hole, which was a quarter-mile from her house. She carried the water in a five-gallon can on top of her head and, even with her limp, she barely spilled a drop.

The silence in the room was beginning to soften. Someone giggled. Someone else spoke. Soon everyone in the audience was talking excitedly, telling jokes, and laughing, including the men on the panel. It was thrilling to watch the light shine in the women's eyes and to see it reflected and multiplied among them. It was as though they all had been a team running a relay and had just found out they had won first place. We loudly applauded ourselves and sailed out of the meeting room feeling giddy, buoyant, joyous.

The rush of pride and sense of awareness I shared with the women that afternoon come back to me at different times during my life today. I think of them when I need a reminder of how human beings everywhere contribute each day to the well-being of our world. This happens whether or not we are recognized for it. This lesson is one of the many gifts given to me while I was a Peace Corps Volunteer in the Dominican Republic.

Dianne Garyantes *(Dominican Republic 1989-1991) lived in El Pozo de Nagua, where she worked on community development projects. She has a graduate degree in public administration and international development from Rutgers University and a B.A. degree in journalism/political science from Pennsylvania State University. She currently works for the Discovery Channel.*

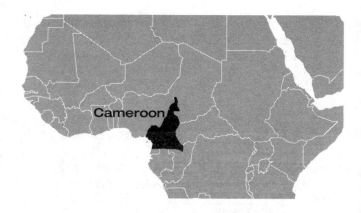

Development Is Down This Road
by Abigail Calkins

Few people recognize me without my familiar Suzuki. Now I have this red Yamaha DT they gave me to replace it. I'm still white, though. Or so they keep insisting as I pass by the shouting voices trying to get me to stop to do a favor, chat, or taste the new palm wine. I know I have a bike, but how do you say "I'm not a taxi" in the local language? I'm late. I'm in a hurry. I've got to help a women's group plant rows of plantains and pineapple in their community farm.

This road could jostle my insides right out of me. My thighs are sore from being abused as shock absorbers. Someone must have made the road longer today; all my landmarks keep reappearing. Didn't I pass that tree already? No, wait, here we go, time to cross the dreaded swamp. Water's high this morning, but I'm pretty sure I can make it through, feet up in the air, water splashing to the sides, engine roaring and … it dies. Damn!

Is it possible to kick-start this thing without putting my feet down? I balance momentarily, contemplating the impossible. Reluctantly, I submerge my wonderful, quickly aging leather boots, feeling them flood, soaking my jeans up to my thighs. I dismount and push the bike through the water to the other side.

I hate this job. I hate this job. I hate this job.

The bathers must wonder about the crazy white woman talking to herself. One little girl is crying because my yellow helmet makes me look like a monster. So I take it off. She starts shrieking. White people are ghosts. White people have funny hair and noses. White people who ride motos with helmets have strange markings of dust on their faces. Unable to pacify the kid, I shove on to the village, which is mercifully close.

The president of the women's group is waiting for me. Sloshing over to her, I pull off my gloves and helmet to embrace her. At last, we can get down to business. Drums sound nearby. Uh-oh . . . not drums! Not again! Not after this hour-and-a-half-drive! Not after crossing the dreaded swamp!

The president leads me to a group of dancing women, each of whom hugs me and invites me to join them in celebration of an old man who lies dead on a cot. We dance, and I try to conceal my discomfort in celebrating death, even that of an old man. No community farms today, folks. Development will have to wait.

When the drums finally stop, the group escorts me rather officially to the president's house. They tell me they want to try making soap. This, after all, is the kind of technical know-how a white woman on a red motorcycle should have. Frankly, I don't have the first clue about soap making.

They unknowingly introduce me to the process: lye, blanched palm oil, and three hours of stirring. The women are singing songs, songs about soap, and my heart lifts as I help them stir. Someone brings me corn on the cob and warm beer. I look around. Such strength! These women with wide, open faces and old but colorful scarves wrapped around their hair, gossiping and laughing and occasionally arguing. I love this job. This job is great. I wouldn't miss this job for the world. You women are wonderful, every one of you; you make your own soap, so what if you won't work on your community farm? Soap classifies as development, doesn't it? Thunder rumbles in the distance.

It is getting late. I say, "Would it bother you if I leave now? I need to return home," and they look bothered and tell me that I must stay until the soap is finished. I oblige helplessly, pushing thunder out of my mind. More singing, stirring, and bickering, but at last the women pour the thick green soap into the square wooden mold and I take out my camera to capture the triumph. (I will say back home, "And this was the day we made soap!")

The group presents me with a gift, a splendid, singular egg, beautiful and simple. It is an egg that I will eat with joy. That is, if it makes it home intact. That is, if I make it home intact. Speaking my local-language thank-yous and good-byes, I return grimly to my red chariot. So we meet again, beast.

The swamp provides no challenge this time, since my socks and jeans are still damp. My fears rest more with the deep, black mass of clouds off to my left. How fast do I have to drive to arrive home before the storm hits? If I go 264 kilometers an hour, I could be in my house in ten minutes. Chickens and children will fly. Cars will flip over behind me, and I will never even hear the fracas. Please don't rain, please don't rain, please don't rain.

The first drops splash on my nose, followed quickly by a torrential downpour, drenching me almost immediately, a cold and cruel rain, seeping beneath my kidney belt, sparing nothing. Wasn't it supposed to be warm in Africa? Swearing through my chattering teeth, I am forced to continue because there is no house in sight. Why do I do this? Why? I laugh in my ridiculous misery.

Finally, I pull into a village where some men are grilling corn on a small fire. They invite me to warm myself by it until the rain subsides. It helps. I stare out at the storm and the road. All the carefree days I glided past this village on dry dirt and never even appreciated my good fortune. Ten kilometers remain between me and my house. Streams of muddy water flood the road, redefining it. Soon it will look like chocolate frosting. Back to the bike, the helmet, and the last drizzle of rain. Home is just around the next few bends.

Abigail Calkins *(Cameroon 1987-1990) was a community development Volunteer in Abong-Mbang, Cameroon, where she worked with women's groups in ten villages. She has an M.A. in public administration/international development from Columbia University and a B.A. in international relations and French from Tufts University.*

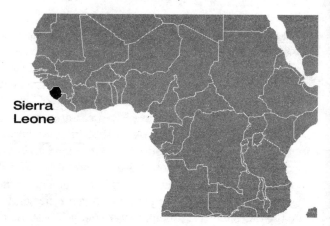

Sierra
Leone

Fishing in Sierra Leone

by Phil Bob Hellmich

During my first fishing trip in West Africa, I realized a childhood dream by fighting and landing a twenty-five-pound Nile perch. That experience changed the rest of my time in Sierra Leone as a Peace Corps Volunteer.

My main project was building a well. During the dry season, I spent the evenings fishing Sierra Leone's Rokel River with my host-country friends, the Conteh brothers—Moses, Bokarie, and Sanpha.

I caught more than 125 pounds of Nile perch a month. My interest in fishing changed as did my diet, which greatly improved with the fresh fish. I soon realized the Conteh brothers had similar enthusiasm for fishing, but the necessity of providing food for their families took precedence over "sport."

I was uncomfortable about using Western fishing lures, commonly referred to by Sierra Leoneans as "English baits," which worked better than the traditional methods

96

of fishing. I was often troubled when I saw Sierra Leoneans embracing Western ways over their own culture and traditions. However, I could not deny the Contehs their attraction for the Western things they had seen since their childhood.

The Conteh brothers had received such lures as presents and used them with hand lines. Most were eventually lost to large perch or the rocky bottom of the Rokel. That was a major loss, since the value of one imported lure was equal to a local teacher's monthly salary.

I lost many myself, and I replaced them from a shop 120 miles from the village. But they were expensive for me, too. Several Peace Corps friends recommended that I make my own. I had never tied a fishing fly, let alone carved a stick into a fishlike lure that could dive and dance in the water. The Contehs had similar doubts, reinforced by a lack of faith in their ability to design and make a fancy "white man's" gadget.

Finally, I set for the Contehs and myself a straightforward goal: to create locally made lures that caught Nile perch and that the Conteh brothers could continue making without me. We set to work together.

The plan was to use only local materials that were readily available. I did not know the local trees and their characteristics, but the Contehs knew the qualities of every tree in the bush and which tree would provide wood with the perfect buoyancy. They relied on their own carving skills to produce their everyday tools. They did not trust me with a knife for fear I would hurt myself.

The process was slow and early attempts failed miserably. Whenever we hit a problem, we would take a few days off until someone came up with an idea of how to use a local material to overcome our obstacle. This process of sharing ideas with one another was called "hanging heads," a Krio expression for group consultation.

The Conteh brothers were slow to develop pride in their work. I was more impressed with the first successful lures than they were. They said the lures were *wo-wo* (ugly). I thought they were beautiful. My Peace Corps friends shared my opinion.

One Volunteer arranged for the Conteh brothers and me to give a workshop for National Park employees. I asked the Contehs to serve as instructors. I hoped that they would gain additional skill at making lures by teaching and that they would serve as an example of Sierra Leoneans being able to make English baits. They were also better at it than I was.

After the workshop, outside interest in the Conteh brothers' work grew. The workshop stirred more discussion within the Peace Corps and the government ministry. The Contehs were still dissatisfied with their own lures and continued to ask me if I would leave them mine when I returned to the United States.

It was during the next workshop, four months later, that the Contehs finally gained a sense of pride.

The workshop came after the rainy season, a period when the Contehs were really too busy with farming to think about lures, and just before the next fishing season.

It was attended by Volunteers and Sierra Leonean development workers from around the country, twenty-one people in all. After the workshop, Moses said, "I did not believe you, Phil Bob, when you said people liked our lures, but when I saw all those important people listening to my every word, my head became bigger than my body."

The Contehs emerged from the workshop with both a sense of pride and a demand for their lures. They returned to their village just as the dry-season fishing began. The "hanging heads" sessions became more frequent as the Contehs began to market lures and to fish. This was when Sanpha returned from the river one night with four Nile perch weighing 101 pounds.

After ten months of making lures, Sanpha was suddenly telling me that he had caught bigger fish than I had, and with lures that he had made himself. He also pointed out that I had never made a single lure from start to finish. We all laughed as I set to work carving my first lure.

Within two months, Bokarie caught several Nile perch—a fish that looks like a large mouth bass—with a lure he made himself.

Over the next twelve months:

- The Contehs became self-sufficient in making lures that attracted Nile perch;
- They began to sell their excess catch for profit; they successfully made their own Western-style fishing reels;
- The Contehs served as trainers in four successful workshops;
- Working together, we also developed lures that caught barracudas and worked well for saltwater fishing;
- And the Contehs started a small business, selling seventy-two lures in three months.

Some while later, during my last fishing trip to the Rokel River, I came across a farmer fishing with a Conteh lure. I quietly sat back and watched as he pulled a Nile perch from the water and headed back to his village. An impossible feat had now become routine, almost casual. It was time to go home.

Phil Bob Hellmich *(Sierra Leone 1985-1989) was a health and rural development Volunteer in Kagbere and Masongbo, Sierre Leone, where he helped to create an appropriate-technology water well project and to develop locally made fishing lures. Hellmich has a B.A. in history from DePauw University.*

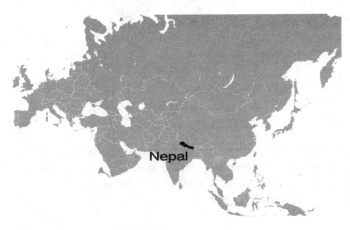

Nepal

Thunder and Enlightenment

by Duane Karlen

Every student in the class looked up at me, waiting for my answer. The room was quiet, unusually quiet for this group of boisterous twelve-year-olds, who rarely sat still on their creaky wooden benches and whose attention often flitted about like the sparrows that came to the open windows.

But today was exam day, and exams are serious business in Nepal. A student's grade can mean the difference between continuing in school or returning to labor in the terraced rice fields that surround the Himalayan mountain village.

Ram Gopal, who had asked the question, was still standing, waiting for permission to resume his seat after addressing the teacher, as was the custom. I told him to sit, adding that I thought his question was a good one, trying to buy a few moments to compose my thoughts. His request was so simple on the surface: "Sir, do you want your answer or our answer on number three?"

I glanced down at the exam: "Briefly explain the cause of thunder and lightning."

I realized Ram's question came from something that had taken place in class a few weeks earlier. We were studying a science unit on weather, concentrating on thunder and lightning. The text gave a rather complicated explanation that involved atmospheric temperature gradients, rising air masses, ionic exchanges, positive and negative electronic discharges, and the speed of light versus the speed of sound. Pretty heady stuff for these young boys and girls who live far from roads and electricity!

I had tried to make the lesson more interesting and understandable by explaining it in simpler words, using demonstrations of static electricity with combs and small bits of paper, and taking the class outside to observe thunderhead clouds forming in the afternoon sky.

This was my second year teaching science in Gahonsahor, an agricultural village two days' walk east of the Pokhara airport. My command of the local alphabet had grown to where I could write on the blackboard to illustrate my diagrams, and my ear for the hill dialect allowed me to follow their discussions about what we were studying. So I was delighted one day when a student bravely asked me, "Sir, would you like to hear our explanation of thunder and lightning?" There was an expectant pause, with all attention on the teacher.

"Yes, tell me!" I replied, making no attempt to act like the traditional teacher who strives to be the sole source of all knowledge and academic wisdom.

What followed was one of the most exciting conversations I have ever heard in a classroom. Students eagerly took turns telling me about Indra, the weather god who lives in the sky. Interrupting and correcting each other in their enthusiasm, they explained how Indra occasionally becomes angry and throws "thunderbolts" down to earth. These flash brilliantly through the sky and strike the ground with a thunderous crash, shattering anything in the way.

These bolts are triangular pieces of rock, rather like very large arrowheads. Usually they are smashed to dust by the impact, the students told me, but once in a while one is found where lightning has struck, black, very hard, smooth like glass on the outside. They are hard to crack, but if you can break off a piece and grind it up, it's a powerful medicine that can cure many problems of the body and spirit.

I asked if anyone had ever seen such a thunderbolt. Most had only heard of them, but a couple of students knew someone who knew someone who had found one, and one student even had an uncle who might actually have one!

I was astonished the next day when one of the students returned to class with a small piece of rock, broken from the original triangle. He excitedly showed it to the entire group, then presented it to me as a gift from his family, to take home and use when necessary. Twenty-five years later, I still keep this treasure in a special brass bowl by my bedside, strong medicine for when I need it.

The science unit on weather had taken several weeks to cover, much longer than the four or five days I had originally scheduled. I was not sure exactly what my students had learned. I would find out from this exam. However, I certainly came away with a feeling of satisfaction that something important had happened.

But now the class was waiting for my answer to Ram's question, and I felt as if I were the one being tested. My reply would tell them how much I understood their culture and accepted what was important to them. Who is "right" here? If the students accept "my" scientific concepts, are they turning their backs on their own heritage? Is my work here then undermining the very cultural uniqueness I have learned to respect? On the other hand, if they assume "their" answer is correct, are they really learning science? I needed a flash of inspiration.

I focused again on my students. There was no ambivalence in their faces. These children were easily able to grasp both sets of beliefs without a problem. One they explored in their classroom; the other was a part of their religion and folklore. Both made sense; both were acceptable. At this moment all they wanted to know was: Which would be the correct answer on the test?

I spoke without further hesitation. "Since this is a science exam, give the scientific explanation. In Hindu culture class, you could give the explanation that involves Indra. But here let's use the one that comes from our textbook."

Relieved at having the issue clarified, the students resumed writing, concentrating on their sentences, occasionally gazing out the window to gather their thoughts. I sat quietly, watching them with fond amazement. Far off in the mountains, signaling the development of an afternoon storm, there was a faint rumble of thunder.

Duane Karlen *(Nepal 1970-1972) taught science and mathematics in a secondary school in rural Nepal. That experience changed his focus of interest from science to human behavior. He went on to a career in counseling, management training, and organizational consulting.*

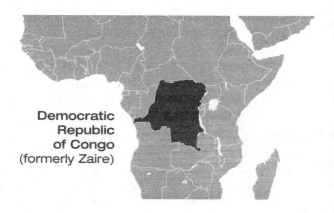

**Democratic
Republic
of Congo**
(formerly Zaire)

The Joy of Digging

by Mike Tidwell

Equipped with a motorcycle from the United States Agency for International Development and administrative support from the Zairian Department of Agriculture and Rural Development, I set out to show the people of Kalambayi something about fish culture. I was an extension agent for the government's Projet Pisciculture Familiale.

Six days a week, I left my house around seven o'clock in the morning and rode as much as forty miles over unspeakably eroded dirt roads and down narrow paths. I visited villages and expounded on the virtues of fish culture to anyone who would listen. "No, thanks," they often said, "we've got enough work to do already." Around six in the evening, exhausted from equal parts of sun and foreign language, I'd return home.

It was after a few weeks of this routine that I met Ilunga Mbumba, chief of the village of Ntita Kalambayi. I was riding my Yamaha 125 Enduro through an uninhabited stretch of bush when he appeared from out of the ten-foot-tall grass along the trail, signaling for me to stop. Even if he hadn't waved, I'm pretty sure I would have stopped anyway. Ilunga had been out hunting antelope and he presented a sight worth inspecting. In one hand he carried a spear, in the other a crude machete. On his head was a kind of coonskin cap with a bushy tail hanging down in back. Around his neck hung a string with a leather charm to ward off evil bush spirits. Two underfed mongrel dogs circled his bare feet, panting.

When I saw Ilunga that first time, I saw a man living, it seemed to me, in another century. Inside the tall grass from which he had just stepped, the clock ran a thousand years slow, if it registered any time at all. Unable to help myself, I openly stared at him, taking him in from head to toe. He, meanwhile, stared back at me with the same wide-eyed incredulity. And no wonder. With my ghost-white skin and rumbling motorcycle, with my bulging safety goggles and orange riding gloves, with my bushy brown beard flowing out from under a banana-yellow crash helmet—with all this, I suppose I had a lot of nerve thinking of him as a museum piece.

For a moment we just kept gawking, Ilunga and I, mentally circling each other, each of us trying to decide whether to burst out laughing or to run for safety. In the end, we did neither. We became friends.

"My name is Ilunga," he said, extending his hand.

"My name is Michel," I said. We shook hands.

We smiled at each other some more before Ilunga got around to telling me he had heard my job was to teach people how to raise fish. It sounded like something worth trying, he said, and he wondered if I would come by his village to help him look for a pond site. I said I would and took down directions to his house.

The next day, the two of us set off into the bush, hunting for a place to raise fish.

"The first thing we need," I told Ilunga, "is water. Do you know a good spot where there's a small stream or a spring?"

"Follow me," he said.

Machetes in hand, we stomped and stumbled and hacked our way through the savanna grass for two hours before finding an acceptable site along a stream about a twenty-minute walk from Ilunga's village. Together, we measured off a pond and staked out a water canal that would run between it and a point farther up the stream. Then, with a shovel I sold him on credit against his next corn harvest, Ilunga began a two-month journey through dark caverns of physical pain and overexertion. He began digging. No bulldozers here. The task of carving out a pond from the valley-bottom floor was left to the farmer himself.

There is no easy way to dig a fish pond with a shovel. You just have to do it. You have to place the tip to the ground, push the shovel in with your foot, pull up a load of dirt, and then throw the load twenty or thirty feet to the pond's edge. Then you have to do it again—tip to the ground, push it in, pull it up, throw the dirt. After you do this about 50,000 times, you have an average-size, ten-by-fifteen-meter pond.

But Ilunga, since he was a chief, wasn't going to be content with an average-size pond. He wanted one almost twice that size. He wanted a pond fifteen by twenty meters. I told him he was crazy as we measured it out. I repeated the point with added conviction after watching him use his bare foot to drive the thin shovel blade into the ground.

"A pond this big is too much work for one person," I said. "It'll kill you."

"See you next week," he said.

"It's too much, Ilunga."

He started digging.

"Okay," I said. *"Bonne chance."*

I left him at the pond site and began heading toward the village, hearing every ten seconds as I walked away the sound of a shovel-load of dirt hitting the ground after traveling twenty feet through the air.

For me, it was painful visiting Ilunga each week. This was the part of the fish-culture process I had been dreading ever since arriving. I'd come by to check on the pond's progress and find Ilunga grunting and shoveling and pitching dirt the same way I had left him the week before. I calculated that to finish the pond he would have to move a total of 4,000 cubic feet of dirt. Guilt gnawed at me. This was no joke. He really was going to kill himself.

One week I couldn't stand it any longer. I found Ilunga at the pond site with his body covered with the usual mixture of dirt and sweat.

"Give me the shovel," I told him.

"Oh no, Michel," he said. "This work is too much for you."

"Give it to me," I repeated, a bit indignantly. "Take a rest."

He shrugged and handed me the shovel. I began digging. Okay, I thought, tip to the ground, push it in, pull it up, throw the dirt. I did it again. It wasn't nearly as hard as I had thought. Stroke after stroke, I kept going. About twenty minutes later, though, it got hot. I began wondering how, at 8:30 in the morning, the sun had suddenly reached noontime intensity. I paused to take off my shirt. Ilunga, thinking I was quitting, jumped up and reached for the shovel.

"No, no," I said. "I'm still digging. Sit down."

He shrugged again and said that since I was apparently serious about digging, he was going to go check on one of his fields. "Good idea," I said.

Shirtless, alone, I carried on. Tip to the ground, push it in, pull it up, throw the dirt. An hour passed. Tip to the ground, push it in, pull it up…throw…throw the…dammit, throw the dirt. My arms were signaling that they didn't like tossing dirt over such a great distance. But I couldn't stop. I had been digging for only an hour and a half. I was determined to go on, to help Ilunga. How could I expect villagers to do work I was incapable of doing myself?

Sweat gathered on my forehead and streamed down my face as I continued, shoveling and shoveling. Another thirty minutes passed and things started to get really ugly. My body buckled with fatigue. My back and shoulders joined my arms in screaming for an end to hostilities. I was no longer able to throw the dirt. Instead, I carried each load twenty feet and ignobly dumped it onto the dike. I was glad Ilunga wasn't around to see this. It was embarrassing. And, God, was it hot—the hottest day I could remember. Even occasional breezes rustling through the surrounding savanna grass didn't help. And then I looked at my hands. Both palms had become blistered. One was bleeding.

I took a short break and then began digging again. The pain resumed, cracking out all over my body. Fifteen minutes later, my hands finally refused to grip the shovel. It fell to the ground. My back refused to bend. I was whipped. After just two hours of digging, I was incapable of doing any more. With a stiff, unnatural walk, I went over to the dike. Ilunga had just returned, and I collapsed next to him.

"I think I'll stop now," I managed, unable to hide my pitiful state. "Take over if you want."

He did. He stood up, grabbed the shovel, and began working—smoothly, confidently, a man inured to hard work. Tip to the ground, push it in, pull it up, throw the dirt. Lying on my side, exhausted, I watched Ilunga. Then I looked hard at the spot where I had been digging. I had done nothing. The hole was essentially unchanged. I had moved perhaps thirty cubic feet of dirt. That meant 3,970 cubic feet for Ilunga.

After the brief digging experience, my weekly visits to the pond became even more painful and my awe of Ilunga grew. Day after day, four or five hours each day, he kept going. He kept digging his pond. He worked like a bull and never complained. Not once. Not when he hit a patch of rocks that required a pickax and extra sweat. Not when, at the enormous pond's center, he had to throw each shovel-load twice to reach the dikes. Not even when he became ill.

His hand was on fire one morning when I arrived and shook it.

"You're sick," I said.

"I know," he said, and resumed digging.

"Then quit working and get some rest."

"I can't," came the reply. "I've got to finish this pond."

Several weeks later, Ilunga drove his shovel into the earth and threw its load one last time. I never thought it would happen, but there it was: Ilunga's pond, huge, fifteen by twenty meters, and completely finished. We hollowed out a bamboo inlet pipe and positioned it in the upper dike so canal water could enter the pond. Three days later, the pond was gloriously full of water. Using my motorcycle and two ten-liter carrying *bidons,* I transported stocking fish from another project post twenty miles to the south. When the last of the 300 tilapia fingerlings had entered the new pond, I turned to Ilunga and shook his hand over and over again. We ran around the banks hooting and hollering, laughing like children, watching the fish and marveling at what a wonderful thing a pond was.

To celebrate, I had brought a bottle of *tshitshampa,* the local home brew, and Ilunga and I began pouring each other shots, slapping each other on the back, and talking entirely too loud for two men sitting alone on a pond bank in the middle of the African bush. A warm glow from the drink spread from our stomachs to our limbs and, soon, strongly, our heads. Ilunga talked about his dream of digging three, six, twelve more fish ponds, and I concluded that there was no biological reason why, if fed properly, tilapia couldn't grow to be the size of Land Rovers. At one point, we decided to assign names to all of Ilunga's fish. Straight-faced, signaling each other to be quiet, we crouched next to the water and began naming the first few fish that swam by. After four fish, though, we lost track of which fish had which names. This struck us as absolutely hilarious, and we fell on our backs and stamped our feet and laughed so hard it hurt.

Oh, sweet joy, the pond was finished. Ilunga had done it. He had taken my instructions and accomplished something important. And on that day when we finally stocked the pond, I knew that no man would ever command more respect from me than one who, to better feed his children, moves 4,000 cubic feet of dirt with a shovel.

Mike Tidwell *(Zaire 1985-1987) is the author of* The Ponds of Kalambayi, *a book about his Peace Corps experience that won the 1991 Paul Cowan Prize given by RPCV Writers & Readers. He is also author of* In the Shadow of the White House: Drugs, Death, and Redemption on the Streets of the Nation's Capital *and* Amazon Stranger. *He is a freelance writer and lives in Takoma Park, Maryland.*

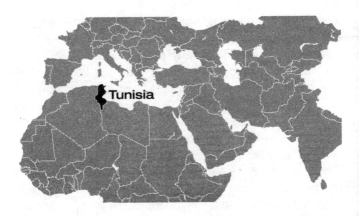

Tunisia

YSWF: Living in an Arab World

by Lora Parisien

Tunisia is steeped in Islam. It is everywhere, in the language, food, daily practice. It is the very fabric of life. Because it is such a dominant force, it cannot be ignored. For the outsider, particularly if the outsider is female, understanding the nature of this force can be a lengthy, arduous process. Men and women in this country are born of a religion—a way of life—that systematically segregates them: separate duties, separate expectations, separate schools, separate rules. There is so much underlying tension about what men and women should or should not be doing, it is no wonder that the mere presence of an outsider is a big snag in the social fabric.

No amount of cross-cultural training could have prepared me for day-to-day life in Tunisia. It is often said by Tunisia's corps of Volunteers, "It is not the physical challenge of living here that is difficult; it is the mental and emotional challenge." I was unprepared to graciously absorb the daily onslaught of propositions I received. In the beginning, I was not sure I would be able to withstand the comments. Depending on my mood, I was tremendously vocal or exceedingly demure. My glow-in-the-dark white skin, my green eyes, my clothing—though archconservative—were indeed Western. My mere presence on the streets invited attention from males of all ages.

I was assigned to the capital, Tunis, a city more crowded than any I have ever known. With 1.6 million residents, Tunis's streets are a teeming mass of people. At first I did not have the nerve to venture outside and explore my neighborhood. I would lie on my bed and stare at the cracked ceiling or the tree I had painted on my wall. I would stay motionless, listening to mopeds whir through the crowded streets of the medina (the traditional walled city) and the constant hammering of the brass smiths outside my window. Cocooned, safe from every possible intrusion, I tried to ignore my obvious lack of courage. When I walked to the Bourguiba Institute where I taught English, a thirty-minute commute, I wore my Walkman for protection. I found listening to the B-52s humorous because the nonsensical music screened out the predictable barrage and put a smile on my face at the same time. Eventually, I abandoned the radio because I began to feel that perhaps it was culturally insensitive. Instead, I counted the number of times I was approached during that thirty-minute trek.

After about six months, something magical happened. I started to feel as if Tunis was my home. Somehow, somewhere along the way, I began to win the war of stares and stopped letting the comments chip away at my personality. I stopped feeling as though every incident was a personal attack in a war waged solely against me. I discovered it was pointless to let these occurrences bother me. A Western woman is fair game and rules don't apply. These exceedingly annoying and overconfident flirtations were just attempts to capture my attention, and my interest. They were also completely harmless. In fact, I was far safer in Tunis than I was in Detroit.

I also enjoyed a powerful tool. I had learned Arabic. Not only was I able to understand the solicitations, but I could respond in the most creative ways! "Now that's not very polite, is it?" Or my favorite, *"Rude bellick, Allah bish yhizz lsaanik."* (Be careful or God's gonna seize your tongue.) Believe it or not, that comment exacted shock and laughter followed by profuse apologies. In training, our instructors had counseled, "Learn the language, learn the language, learn the language." Arabic not only met my basic communication needs, but was my first line of defense.

Once the language barrier started to dissipate, I began to see past my own comfort zone and my eyes opened to a culture much bigger and far more fascinating than I. I began to put things in perspective. I relaxed and found Tunisia to be infinitely complicated and fascinating. I became absorbed in the culture. In *Beyond the Veil,* Fatima Merniss writes:

"The Islamic Veil originated in 18th century Samaria. It was worn by Samarian women to symbolize a woman's freedom—that she should not be assaulted because she is shielded by the veil. Without the veil, she is tempting the man to think about sex. With the veil she saves him from the opportunity to have bad thoughts."

In Tunisia, married women typically wear the *saf-sari* (veil) covering from head to toe. Unmarried women can choose to conform to this code or not. It is often viewed as being submissive not only to God but also to men. What most Western women fail to understand is the freedom offered by a veil. Donning the shapeless sheet does not convey that women are not equal. A woman who chooses to veil is a woman who is convinced by Allah's word as it is written in the Koran, the holy book of Islam. It extends the idea of protection by secluding her in the holy world of Islam. She is not to be bothered. She is not fair game. She has made a conscious decision. Younger women in Tunisia are veiling. This, for the most part, is political in support of fundamentalism. There are some, though, who feel early the pangs of Islam. I had a Tunisian family who "adopted" me. There were three sisters. Besma was my closest friend. She was free-spirited and rejected the veil. Her sisters, ages fifteen and twenty-two, were very devoted to Islam— and very veiled. They even refused to let me see their hair (though they boasted that it was far more beautiful than mine) because I was not a Muslim.

Because Besma refused to veil, they could neither comprehend their middle sibling nor tolerate her. Besma was not rejecting the presence of Allah in her life. She was expressing her desire to have an identity, not hide it. Long walks, arm in arm, through the crowded alleyways of our jam-packed neighborhood put the daily struggles of life in perspective for both of us and gave us respite from our more serious sisters.

Very late one evening, there was a knock at my door. It was rapid and continuous.

I yelled, *"Shkoon?"* (Who is it?)

"Besma," came the reply. *"Fsa, fsa."* (Hurry up.) I opened the door. "You must come over to my house right now, please."

"What's wrong?"

"My mother wants to see you and dinner is waiting."

Although it was late, I was accustomed to these impromptu invitations to meals at the Tounsi household. I changed out of my shorts and T-shirt and into an ankle-length skirt and loose, flowing shirt. We walked hurriedly through the narrow streets, in and out of the complicated labyrinth of the medina to her neighborhood. We knocked on her door in the same manner and heard her mother say, *"Shkoon?"*

"Besma and Noora." (Noora was my Tunisian name.)

The door opened and I was flooded with kisses by Besma's mother, Laila. She seemed especially excited to see me. She held my hand and escorted me through the courtyard into the family living area.

When I entered the tiny chamber that served as a dining room, recreation area, and bedroom, the roomful of waiting people stood up to welcome me. Each came up to me, one by one, and planted the customary four kisses—two per cheek—on my face. I recognized almost everyone in the room as family. The only person not to greet me was an older gentleman, who did not move from his seat but fixed his stare on me from the moment I came in the room. He seemed amused. Besma's mother once again grabbed my hand and led me to the couch, never releasing my fingers from her tight grip. I was seated facing the stranger and the room became very quiet.

Then the stranger started to speak. In perfect English, with a strong Arabic accent, he introduced himself as Uncle Mohammed. He gave me an abbreviated life story. He told me he was educated and that he "took" a degree in dentistry. He was financially secure and could promise me frequent vacations in Europe and a yearly trip to America to see my family. He explained that he had seen a picture of me—one that I had given to Besma. He knew the moment he saw it that I should be his wife. And … did I accept?

Dumbfounded, I looked around the room. Everyone was perched on the edges of their chairs. Except for Mohammed and me, no one in the room could understand English, so they were anxiously awaiting my reaction. I shot Besma a "what-have-you-done-to-me" look. When I turned to Laila, who had now deprived my fingers of blood flow for nearly ten minutes, she was frantically nodding her head yes, yes, yes! I looked back at Mohammed, who was waiting for my favorable reply. "How old are you?" I asked.

"Forty-six," he replied.

"Wow" was all I could say.

"It's a wonderful opportunity for you," he said. "Really, the chance of a lifetime." Then Laila chimed in. "You will be in our family. I am so happy." She was already congratulating me.

"Besma, can I speak with you a moment?" I asked. Besma followed me into the courtyard.

"Really, Besma, he is only four years younger than my father. Too old for me, way too old. Could you marry someone twice your age?"

"No. I'm sorry. Everyone thinks it is such a perfect arrangement. You're alone here. What was I going to say? Don't worry. I thought you might not want to. Tell him it's impossible." Great. How was I going to gracefully decline without offending my Tunisian family? In their eyes, it was as though Mohammed had handed me the keys to a brand-new Ferrari and said, "Here, take it, it's yours." Who would say no to such an offer? We returned to the room. Everyone was prepared to jump right out of their chairs. I sat across from Mohammed.

"I am sorry I cannot accept your gracious offer. My family wants me to marry a man from my hometown, one I have known since childhood." It was a blatant lie. "He is waiting for my return. I am here because there is so much yet to learn. I want to be ready for marriage and right now I am not. I am too young. But when I am ready, it will have to be him I marry."

"I understand," he replied. "Thank you."

With that he got up and exited the room. Laila stared at me with puppy dog eyes and everyone in the room fell back into their chairs, defeated. Besma later explained my reasons. My Tunisian family seemed to accept them without question.

I feel very fortunate to have served in an Islamic country. Two years couldn't possibly have afforded me the time needed to fully grasp the complexity of this rich and mysterious culture. It happened to me, and I watched it happen to my fellow Volunteers—curiosity caught us. We struggled not to escape but to reach an understanding. Through our work, our friendships, our mere presence, we forged an understanding of ourselves and our hosts.

Lora Parisien *(Tunisia 1989-1991) was an English teacher at the Bourguiba Institute for Modern Languages at the University of Tunis. She spent her first year teaching in the capital city, Tunis, and her second in the western city of Beja. Parisien has a B.A. in journalism from Central Michigan University.*

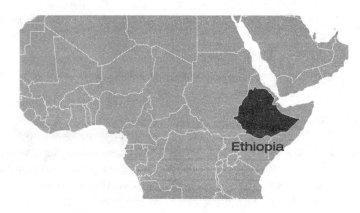

The Right Way to Grow Tomatoes

by Karen DeWitt

I'd forgotten that I had even taken the Peace Corps recruitment test when that long-distance call came on a cold January day in 1965. Then, standing in a battered wooden telephone booth in my dormitory at Miami University of Ohio, I heard someone say, "Congratulations. You've been accepted."

Suddenly graduate school, a job, the ordinary future that stretched before me and my classmates disappeared, replaced by adventure, excitement, and the unknown—literally the unknown, for I hadn't even asked what country I would be stationed in. Didn't know, didn't care.

Suddenly, I was to be part of an adventure for my generation. I was to become a Kennedy kid, one of those thousands of young people whom he had asked to dedicate one or two years of their lives to work in Africa, Latin America, or Asia.

It was a heady invitation, asking not what your country could do for you, but what you could do for your country. Here was something I could do.

According to the television commercials, the Peace Corps involved scrabbling up hills and swinging across ravines in Marine-style training, laughing with exotically dressed peoples, speaking in strange tongues, teaching, drilling wells, living in mud houses. Hey—now that was me!

The first letter from the Peace Corps told me I was going to Turkey. Great. I'd never been to Turkey. A second letter corrected the first; I was going to India. Cool. A third letter said East Africa—Ethiopia, to be specific. Wonderful. I found Ethiopia on a map, then sought out the sole Ethiopian student on campus. He was amused by my enthusiasm. Only a short while ago I hadn't known he existed. Now I was fumbling around in his language, ravenous for information about his culture and customs.

The Peace Corps did a great job of training me. Eighteen months after that telephone call, with three months of living and teaching in the "culturally different" East Los Angeles barrio, and a month of in-country training under my belt, I was a teacher of English. And thanks to months of language training, I arrived in the highland village of Ghion armed with a great deal of Amharic, Ethiopia's national language, though that never prevented me from saying the word "yellow" when I meant "only."

I had expected, in my arrogance and ignorance, that I would give more than I got. I didn't. And my life has been the richer for it. I learned things profound and mundane: that a real "free-range" chicken is a tough bird to fry; that you get a heap of liver from a freshly slaughtered cow; that growing tomatoes in a frame is far superior to staking them, as I'd always been taught; that Africa is mighty cold at 8,000 feet above sea level; that I had a gift for teaching.

As a student, I confess I was less successful. In an effort to quit smoking, I decided to learn to spin cotton. A deft Ethiopian woman named Conjeet tried for months to teach me, but never quite succeeded. Holding her spindle—which looked like an old-fashioned wooden baby rattle—in one hand, and darting it in and out of a puff of cotton, Conjeet spun threads as fine as any I'd ever pulled from a commercial spool. It looked so easy. I spun rope, I spun twine, I spun cord, I spun cable, but I never produced a thread as fine as Conjeet's. Her friends would come night after night to watch the *ferenji* (foreign woman) spin, giggling at my efforts. They were sure I'd never get a husband.

"You spin like a man," laughed Conjeet. And so, instead of the sheer white shawl worn by Ethiopian women, the village weaver made a *gabi,* a heavy man's garment, from my thread. I wore it the whole time I was in Ethiopia.

I had great admiration for much that I met with in Ethiopia. But I never tried to become Ethiopian, because there was always some aspect of the culture that didn't suit me. I was an incurable American.

Shortly after my arrival in Ghion, my neighbor, Ato Getachew, an important landlord in the area, invited me for a meal and did something that horrified me. He picked among the leftover bones from the stew we had eaten, and with the hauteur of a king, offered one to his son. The boy shuffled forward, eyes lowered, his left hand politely holding the wrist of his outstretched right hand.

The boy scuttled back to his corner to gnaw on the bone like a dog. This was a perfectly acceptable way to treat a child by traditional Ethiopian standards, but it shocked me.

However, I did encounter developing world justice in a very satisfactory form on an Ethiopian bus. Buses were always crowded, and in order to make a second run back to the capital before nightfall, the buses on my route often doubled up passengers from one bus to another at a village halfway to Ghion. The little Russian-built buses had a capacity of thirty passengers, but there were often twice as many people crammed aboard. Women and children were the first to suffer. Ousted from their seats, they ended up on the floor as men jammed into their places. I'd seen this many times, but on this day I shouted to the driver that this was unjust, illegal, and unsafe. He laughed. Frustrated, I told him that he could do what he liked but the farmer who sat beside me and I were going to be the sole occupants of our seat.

At that moment, a well-filled-out man of status, a *teliq saw* (important man), clambered onto the bus, the last to board. He surveyed the passengers. He shoved the poor farmer away and took his seat. I told the *teliq saw* he could not do that. He laughed at me. He said he was a lawyer from Addis Ababa. Using an informal Amharic reserved for children and servants, he told me to mind my own business.

I let my great-granny's Irish temper get the best of me. I told him a good many things about himself, and then I suggested he get up. He laughed again. I stabbed the tip of my umbrella into his thigh.

He got up. He stayed up. The poor farmer, far from thankful at the return of his seat, balanced nervously at its far edge, as far away from the crazy *ferenji* as possible.

Until the bus pulled into Ghion, the lawyer lectured the passengers on the evils of Peace Corps Volunteers, the low morals of American women, the bad examples we were to his country's women and children, and how we had no jobs in the United States and had come to Ethiopia to eat meat every day. He was going to have me put into jail, he announced.

When the bus reached Ghion, the lawyer grabbed my arm and told me that I was going to the police station. I shook him off. He grabbed me again. Right there in the middle of Ghion's main thoroughfare, that lawyer and I began fighting. I slashed away at him with my umbrella, like some mad, black Mary Poppins. By now, it was night, the hour of the evening stroll, and we attracted a crowd, including many students from my school. Eventually we attracted the police.

Lawyer, police, crowd, and I went off to the police station. After much discussion, the police jailed the Addis lawyer. He wasn't from the town. I was.

The Amharic word I heard most often during my time in Ethiopia was *ferenji*—foreign woman. Whether spoken affectionately or harshly, the word reminded me that I was in the country but not of it. No matter that I was fluent in the local language, ate only local food, was godparent to a villager's child and buddy to the local moonshiner, I was still the foreigner. But that wasn't true that night. I was the *yesalem guad* (Peace Corps) from Ghion. I belonged there, and the out-of-town lawyer did not.

The next day, my students wanted to know how I dared to do what I had done. I was a woman; he was a man. True, I was a teacher, a position with status, but he was a lawyer. I lived in a little provincial village, while he was from the capital. I was young then, so I used the incident to teach a lesson in democracy, the principles of social equality, and respect for the individual within the community, regardless of status and power.

I don't know whether I did them a favor or not. I don't know if the experience wasn't more valuable to me than to the local people. I don't even know, now, if I acted with the best motives—standing up against injustice—or whether I wasn't just an ignorant and arrogant American, annoyed at being inconvenienced.

What I do know is that the whole experience made me adventurous and eager for more. For more culture, more countries, more languages, more roads and vistas, more smells, sounds, and experiences beyond those of my own country. My years in the Peace Corps gave me a perspective from which to understand different attitudes toward time, and to understand that there is more than one right way to do things, including growing tomatoes.

Karen DeWitt *(Ethiopia 1966-1968) has been a producer for* Nightline *at ABC News and a reporter for the* Washington Post, USA Today, *and the* New York Times. *She currently is a free-lance writer in Washington, D.C.*

Goods and Services

by Larissa Zoot

For a couple of weeks I was content to sit and wait patiently, watching the light bulb flicker on and off. At first it took ten minutes, then twenty, thirty, forty-five, and finally it would be more than an hour before the connection was made and the light stayed on in my room. When it reached one hour, I lost my patience and just didn't bother turning it on anymore.

I got by this way for several weeks, going to bed early or hanging out at the neighbors' instead of spending the evening in my unlighted house. Getting ready for bed only took a few minutes and it was easy to do by candlelight. I had lived that way for six months before the electricity came, so there was no reason why I shouldn't have been able to keep living that way.

Then something strange and unexpected happened. I began having a lot of work to do, more work than I could finish before the sun went down in the afternoon. Electric light became a necessary resource, so I had to track down an electrician.

The "electrician" turned out to be a young newlywed who lived just down the street. He showed up at my door late one afternoon with a screwdriver and a roll of electrical tape and started taking things apart. I'm sure he had no training or formal knowledge of electrical systems, so I held my breath, crossed my fingers, and tried to be of use, handing him parts when he needed them and otherwise staying out of his way.

That evening he could not find the flaw or fix it, but he came back early the next day. This time he took a few more things apart, found the problem, and fixed it. Once he had the light fixture put back together and I had tested it several times to make sure it worked, I smiled contentedly, following him to the door, and asked the standard question: "How much do I owe you?"

The reply I received was also standard. "Nothing. Just your thanks." No money. No goods in trade. Not even a beer or a soda. Just thanks. So I offered him my most grateful, enthusiastic "Thank you!" and then watched him disappear down the street.

This is something I've experienced many times now in Alubaren, and it always leaves me stumped. Doesn't he realize that what he just did for me is considered work? Doesn't he know that his time and effort have value? Doesn't he need every penny he can get to provide for his new wife and baby?

Obviously he's not aware that back at home in the United States I would have paid through the nose for the services of an electrician, or for any other work I needed to have done. Is it possible he doesn't recognize that I'm one of the highest-paid people in this town overshadowed by poverty, and I would gladly hand over whatever amount he chose to request? Or does he realize all of this, and it is I who's missing the point?

I think over some of the other times I've experienced this phenomenon: the bus driver who hauled my new furniture over from the next village when the Volunteer there left; the seamstress who took in the waists of my shorts when I lost too much weight and they were falling down; the carpenter who carried my new bookshelf down the mountainside on his back; the mayor's secretary who typed up an official letter that I needed to send to the Ministry of Health; the teacher who took my packages to the post office on her weekend in the capital; and the neighbor who lets me cook on her stove anytime I want to, but won't ever let me buy firewood.

And there are more. What is it with all of these people who are so kind and do so much for me, but never accept any payment or ask for anything in return? Is it because I'm the gringa, an outsider, and they want to give a good impression of their people and their country? Do they intend to create that good impression by treating me extra special?

That's what I thought at first, but with time I realized that I'd been mistaken. It seems to have been another case of my seeing things through the filter of my North American values.

Now I've been in Alubaren long enough to gain a truer perspective on how things work here. The bus driver runs errands for people all the time and never charges a penny. A person who has coconuts or mangoes growing in her backyard will give them away to a neighbor who doesn't have them, but needs them for a recipe, and not even expect a sample of the finished product. A seamstress will stay up all night long making school uniforms for the children of another mother who doesn't have a sewing machine. It's just the way they are.

I hope that this generosity, this sense of community, is something I'll be able to take back with me. I hope I can remember it and practice it, at least to some extent. There's something very special about a place where the primary "value" placed on goods and services is the people's value for one another.

Larissa Zoot *(Honduras 1993-1995) was a child survival Volunteer in Alubaren, Francisco Morazan, Honduras, where she worked with midwives, volunteer health workers, and community groups in seven villages. Zoot is currently working on a master of public health in health management and policy at the University of Michigan, and has a B.S. in community health education from the University of Wisconsin at LaCrosse.*

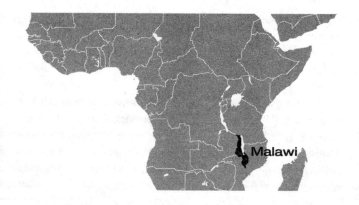

Family Affair

by Tana Elizabeth Beverwyk

Sargent Shriver, first Director of the Peace Corps, liked to say that the real beneficiaries of the Peace Corps would be the children of Volunteers. He meant that former Volunteers would raise their children differently because of the experience. Little did Shriver realize, back in the early 1960s, that for many families Peace Corps service itself would become a legacy. Someday the kids might inherit the family business, the attic antiques, even the homestead. But first, maybe, they'd join the Peace Corps.

The Peace Corps has found over the years that it is former Volunteers who make the best recruiters, and they are especially successful at recruiting other family members. Having a member of one's own family not only recommend the Peace Corps but also tell stories and show slides makes the experience very up close and personal.

The Great Adventure

This essay demonstrates what can happen when a Volunteer travels in Africa with her parents who served in the Peace Corps there twenty-six years earlier. — Editors

I am serving as a Volunteer in Malawi, a small nation in southeastern Africa. Several months ago I traveled to the capital, Lilongwe, to meet my father, mother, and older sister, who were coming for a visit. However, this was no ordinary visit, since my family had left Africa twenty-six years ago and was returning for the first time.

My mother and father had both served as Peace Corps Volunteers in Kenya from 1969 to 1970. They were newlyweds. My sister was born during their time of service. (Peace Corps policy was a little more relaxed about pregnant Volunteers back then.) Those two years in the Peace Corps changed my parents' lives and, subsequently, changed my own. Everything, from their decision to make a home in northern New Mexico because it looked and felt like East Africa to raising their children as global citizens, resulted from their time working as secondary-school teachers in Kenya.

The first part of our time together here in Malawi was spent exploring. It was wonderful to share with them the beauty of Malawi and its people. They were sharply reminded of the unique life of a Volunteer: the lonely silence of a rural village, the frustrating cross-cultural struggles at work, the stress-relieving parties that erupt when Volunteers get together. All of this took them back to a time when they, too, ran to jump on a crowded country bus and struggled with this life they had chosen.

The apex of their homecoming to Africa, however, was our journey to a tiny village in Nyanza Province of south-western Kenya. Taran'ganya was the place where they had lived and served as Volunteers so many years ago. Their first contact with the past was with a former student they had taught as Volunteers, now a highly respected professor in Nairobi, who had kept in contact throughout the years. He opened his home to us with great pride, having, as he sincerely said, "finally the chance to give back a little of what his Peace Corps teachers had given to him."

He took over all the arrangements for our trip to Kuria District to visit Taran'ganya Secondary School and many of his former classmates. The 350-mile trip was filled with memories for my parents: the dirt roads where they had desperately hitched rides when they were my age; the market where they bought bananas, powdered milk, and, occasionally, fresh meat; the people speaking a mix of Kiswahili, Kikuria, and English. For my sister and me, it provided a sharp realization of the impact that those two years had had on our parents, as well as proof that the Peace Corps adventure stories we had grown up hearing were, indeed, true.

Their region had changed and prospered in twenty-six years, just like the rest of Kenya. Their small school was now twice the size it had been in 1969. Its whitewashed buildings housed hundreds of anxious-faced students still learning out of old, dingy textbooks. As we walked into the schoolyard, students and teachers excitedly rushed out to see why the four *wazungu* (white people), accompanied by the well-known professor, were visiting their school. My parents were beaming as they spoke with these students who were so much like those they had taught, in that same small place, twenty-six years before.

The Great Adventure

We spent the next three days in Kuria visiting former students who had remained in their tribal district. I wish I could describe the rush of emotions experienced by Mom and Dad. To see their former students, schoolboys who could barely afford a pair of shoes, as professional adults with grown families was quite overwhelming for them.

The first student we visited was now the chief of a major Kuria village. He cried out with amazement at seeing his teachers again, and, over warm Fanta and biscuits, told stories about how my parents had changed his life. He spoke of spending hours at their house reading Mark Twain. He thanked them for their influence on his decision not to have his six daughters sent for female circumcision, still widely practiced among the Kuria people. My parents had no idea that their influence had been so profound on the quiet boy who would read in their house until the paraffin lamp ran out of fuel. It was so profound, in fact, that he had grown into an influential man who would begin, by daring example, to end a harmful practice among his people.

We then visited another former student who had become a successful doctor. He had chosen to stay in his town to practice medicine and to build a hospital, the region's first. Never have I seen the eyes of a grown man light up as much as his when he realized who the gray-haired people standing before him were. He was chattering immediately about the powerful influence Mom and Dad had had on him. He talked about the boxing and track clubs dad had started, and attributed the fact that he now writes in only capital letters to his trying to emulate the writing of his old Peace Corps teacher. He could hardly believe that the twenty-five-year-old woman in front of him was the same tiny baby to whom he and his friends had brought gifts when she was born. She was the first white baby they had ever seen.

On our way back to Nairobi, we stopped at a small public health clinic in the town of Migori to visit the old medical assistant who had worked in the village near the school. He had given my father an injection to treat a bout of malaria twenty-six years ago. After the usual tears and delighted chatter, he took my mom's hand and led her to the back of the clinic. There he produced a medical text that she had given him as a gift before her tour in the Peace Corps ended. For all these years, it was the only training manual for the laboratory staff of the clinic. The book was now tattered and torn but was still serving a purpose my mother could not have imagined when she passed it on.

The point of these reflections is that my parents had absolutely no idea how much influence they were having during their two years of Peace Corps service. They did not consider themselves exceptional Volunteers; they simply went to class, taught a variety of subjects in the best way they knew how, and loved the people they lived among. But returning to their village so many years later, they were struck by the undeniable realization that they had indeed changed people's lives.

Seeing how these former students reacted to my parents was incredible, persuasive evidence that Peace Corps Volunteers have a profound influence wherever they go, whatever they do. In fact, I felt that a Volunteer could almost spend the entire two years of service locked inside a house and still change something significant in the lives of people all around.

Tana Elizabeth Beverwyk *(Malawi 1995-1998) was an AIDS education Volunteer in Mpherembe, Malawi. She has a B.A. in communications arts and sciences from Michigan State University.*

Paraguay

May the Circle Be Unbroken

by John Garamendi

At the customs area in the Asunción Airport, I wait anxiously for my luggage, loaded down with Christmas presents. At last, I pass through customs and greet my son, John, and his wife, Colleen, who are in Paraguay as Peace Corps Volunteers. We hug and kiss, even shed a few tears. I am proud of them and the commitment they've made. I'm glad to see them and eager to find out firsthand about their lives.

In a cab, we ride past fancy suburbs with high walls, past big houses and European and American stores and auto dealerships, to the old town, with its narrow streets, dirty gutters, and crumbling sidewalks. We enter the Shara Hotel, a Peace Corps crash house. Six bucks per person, a good price even if it doesn't include a working air conditioner.

I remember my own days as a Peace Corps Volunteer thirty years ago in Ethiopia: cheap hotels in the old quarter of Addis Ababa; slow-moving ceiling fans stirring humid air; noisy patrons at the local bars across the street; narrow beds with thin mattresses that sagged like the backs of old donkeys carrying water in the village. Memories of Patti, my wife, a bright-eyed, eager woman lying next to me, unable to sleep as she analyzes the problems of our village and conjures up answers that dissolve in the swish, swish, swish of the fan blades overhead. But hope is miraculously restored the next morning. We awake eager to return to the village, to seize the day and get on with the towering task.

The next morning, John and Colleen show me Asunción, filling me in on its history, and I remember how Patti and I escorted my own parents through Addis Ababa when we were Volunteers. We, too, gave my parents a similar lecture.

To reach John and Colleen's village, I suggest we hire a car, but John shakes his head: "We'll take the bus, Dad. They wouldn't understand if we came in a car."

Of course, in Ethiopia years ago, his mother and I did not have the luxury of renting a car either, nor would our villagers have understood if we arrived by Land Rover.

On the bus out of the capital, we travel through green, rolling country, passing the occasional small, tin-roofed house with a red dirt yard where children play football with deflated balls. When the bus stops, roadside vendors yell to catch our attention, holding up boxes of soda and candy.

At Caaquazu, three hours out of Asunción on the road to Brazil, we leave the bus again and unload our luggage. Colleen dashes to the *supermercado* while John negotiates with taxi drivers to take us the last sixteen kilometers to Sextilinnia, their village. At first, negotiations do not go well. The drivers protest. The road is impassable, they say.

But my son's negotiating skills slowly overcome their reluctance and, finally, a driver agrees to give it a try.

Soon after leaving the paved streets of Caaquazu, we hit a deep sea of mud. Our driver swings past the pool, carving a new road across a field. We continue on, forging new tracks where necessary. We are halfway to Sextilinnia when the driver, his wheels churning hopelessly, surrenders: *"No mas,"* he sighs.

Fortunately, there is a truck nearby belonging to people John and Colleen know—John, in fact, is building a water system for the school in their village—and they agree to drive us the rest of the way.

The village of Sextilinnia has only five houses. Corn and manioc plants grow in the rich soil that John tells me is fifty meters deep, thanks to runoff from the Andes. Years ago, in an attempt at land reform, the government gave the *campesinos* forested land, some tools, and a bit of hope. Now the forests are nearly gone, and the Ministry of Agriculture failed in an effort to cultivate citrus trees. The grind of poverty and subsistence farming goes on and on.

We unload the truck and carry the luggage into the house. "We can't let the neighbors know we have all this," John says. "They wouldn't understand such wealth."

After they open their presents, they take me on a tour of their village. Up the hill is the school where Colleen teaches health classes and John has undertaken a construction project. Beyond the hill we visit families. "This woman just had twins," Colleen explains, pointing to one house. "That was a month ago. I got her to the clinic in time to save the second child and the mother." She smiles sadly, remembering the event. "This is my work," she whispers.

And then my son continues, "Their father is my counterpart. He's a hoot. A strong leader. I took him into Asunción for counterpart day a few months ago, and he was so distracted he forgot to pay the school electric bill. That might cost him the PTA presidency," he explains, laughing.

We continue along the road, exchanging greetings with everyone who passes. We stop to talk with a strawberry farmer. "Too much rain, the crop is no good," he says as we sit under a barren citrus tree in his red earth patio. "But come see my latrine. I'm building it just like you said, away from the water well."

The two men stand on the mound of fresh earth and stare into the newly dug pit. Both voices speak with pride about the depth of the hole. We stay some time beneath the citrus tree. They talk of crops, children, the new school building, of health, of family, and of hope. The exchange is joyful, happy, boisterous, and good.

Later, back at the house, we sit on the porch, slapping ants that crawl up our legs and taking bets on when it will start to rain.

Eventually, it's time for bed and my son warns me, "Oh, if it rains really hard, you might want to move your bed over to that spot." He points across the room. "That's the only place in this room where it doesn't drip."

Shortly after midnight, a rooster is confused by the lightning and thunder and starts crowing. Down the hill another joins him. Soon roosters from the whole village are answering back.

At 5:45 a.m. the alarm rings. I knock on my son's door. Go back to sleep, he tells me. There will be no bus today. We'll have to walk to the main road.

When everyone is up, we shut down the house, load our packs, cover them with rubber rain gear, and head off on the sixteen-kilometer hike to Caaquazu and the bus to Asunción. It keeps raining and the mud gets deeper. There is no bus. No jeeps. Not even an oxcart. The three of us trek on, keeping up our spirits by claiming to have the heaviest pack, to be the wettest. We stop at the house of another Peace Corps Volunteer, who offers us coffee and dry clothes. Like all Volunteers, thirty years ago and today, what we have, we share.

Back in the capital, we sit and talk most of the night. We reform the Peace Corps, straighten out the Department of the Interior where I work, restructure the White House, as well as the Paraguayan government. There is no problem we can't solve.

Thirty years ago, my wife and I talked the same talk. We had solutions to the problems of Ethiopia, the United States, and the world. Now I wonder: Did we do any good as Peace Corps Volunteers in Ethiopia? Will John and Colleen do any good in Paraguay?

The answer, I think, is in the smiles and laughter of those we left behind in our highland village and in our own lives, and what we made of each day's work. The answer is also the children that we raised—for us, a son who cares enough about solving the problems of the world to join the Peace Corps. The answer is the work that Colleen and John are doing today in Paraguay—the same kind of work Patti and I did in Ethiopia thirty years ago.

There's a country-and-western song that says it best: May the circle be unbroken. That's the answer. May the circle of helping others go unbroken. In Paraguay, with my son and daughter-in-law, I realized I had come full circle. I had come home again to the Peace Corps.

John Garamendi *(Ethiopia 1966-1968) graduated from the University of California, Berkeley, where he was an All Pacific Coast Conference football player. After serving in the Peace Corps and earning an M.B.A. from Harvard University, he began a 20-year legislative career in the state of California. In 1995, he was appointed by President Clinton to serve as Deputy Secretary of the Interior. Today, he is in private business.*

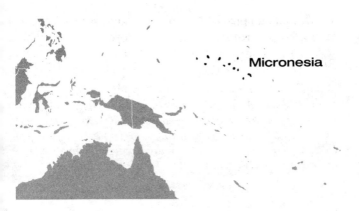

Micronesia

Everyone Everywhere Has Tales to Tell

by Carol Severance

One of the more extraordinary trips I experienced while a Peace Corps Volunteer in Micronesia was on the trading vessel Maria Carmela. I needed to travel from my home island of Ettal in the lower Mortlocks of Chuuk (formerly Truk) to the district center one hundred fifty miles away. The trip took five days.

Because Ettal had no pass into the lagoon, all loading of seagoing vessels took place via outrigger paddling canoes. We passengers and all of our gear bobbed up and down on the ocean swells as we waited to climb aboard the larger Maria Carmela. The climb itself was very awkward for those of us wearing skirts, the only acceptable dress for outer-island Chuukese women.

Aboard, the weathered deck of the Carmela trembled with each throb of its engine and the fetid odor of diesel fumes rode heavily on the humid, tropical air.

The captain pushed his way through the colorful crowd attempting to prepare his vessel for departure. He shouted orders to passengers and crew, and at last the visitors clambered over the side and back into their canoes. The engine rumbled louder, and we were on our way.

The deck of the hand-hewn Carmela was thirty-nine feet long. There were forty-eight men, women, and children aboard as it traveled away from Ettal. There were also thirteen hens, a rooster, and a litter of pigs.

Freshly caught tuna hung from the mast and hundreds of green drinking coconuts filled the deck and wheelhouse. Even the engine room had its share.

When I asked if anyone had ever been lost overboard on a moonlit night, the captain glanced around the crowded deck, grinned, and said, "I have no idea."

The trip itself was filled with storytelling, singing, and laughter. I heard traditional tales of caution and wonder, and gossip unending about islanders from near and far.

Favorite among the stories were those about local Peace Corps Volunteers. Like the couple who had become so upset when the case of toilet paper they had ordered was lifted soaking wet from the bottom of the ship's hold. What could they possibly want with that big box of wet paper, my shipboard companions wanted to know. The islanders often competed with stories about their Volunteers—who could speak the language best, who could sing, or sew, or paddle a small canoe without tipping it over.

I sat blushing through a tale of bravery I had unwittingly created when a sailing canoe on which I'd been a passenger had passed directly over two sleeping whales. Never mind that I didn't know at the time what the whales were and had thus hung curiously over the side to inspect them as we passed.

"If the whales had awakened, they would have played with the canoe," the storyteller assured his audience. "The whales wouldn't have hurt the people, but after they left, the sharks would have."

The story brought slowly shaking heads and many clicking tongues. Ettal was fortunate to have such a fearless American among them, the listeners agreed. Only a few grinned openly.

The weather remained calm and placid throughout the voyage, a blessing to the Chuukese women, who assured me they would otherwise have been quite seasick the entire way. For the same reason, I was more than happy to be sailing on a summer-smooth sea. Dolphins paced the Carmela from time to time, leaping and spinning, racing ahead, then dropping back to ride the bow wave. We saw giant sea turtles and schools of flying fish, but no whales. That resulted in another telling of my fearless whale adventure. I noticed a number of added details the second time around.

I was an artist when I entered the Peace Corps, and I took my paints and brushes so that I could document my stay. I hadn't counted on the ants eating the sealant off my carefully stretched canvases, or on the vivid tones of the tropics. My pallet included colors better suited to landscapes near my Colorado home.

So I began writing down the scenes I wished someday to paint—describing the giant breadfruit tree outside my house, the low sweep of green surrounding the pristine blue of Ettal Lagoon, the faces of laughing children.

In the meantime, I listened to the stories the islanders told. As my language skills grew, I began to recognize how they turned simple news into anecdotes to capture their listeners' interest and, when a story proved worth retelling, added more and more colorful details. In my journal, I began adding details, too—sounds and smells, tastes and textures. My tales grew more complex. By the time I left, my words provided a much clearer image of the islands than my paintings ever could.

I have continued to write since that time. I trained and worked as a journalist first, then returned to telling stories of the islands. Now I write novels and short stories and plays, based most frequently on Pacific Island lore and lifestyle. When I read from my first novel, *Reefsong,* on the University of Hawaii at Hilo campus, a group of Chuukese students came to listen. They grinned at recognized settings and events, and laughed freely at my island characters' foibles. I felt as if I were back on the Maria Carmela.

I can still smell the diesel fumes and the thick pungency of fresh-roasted copra that rode with us on that trip. In fact, I can still hear the captain's panicked call on the last day when the steering chain suddenly jammed. We were just entering the Chuuk Lagoon and were in serious danger of going aground. There was a mad scramble as chickens and children and piglets and fish were passed from hand to hand to clear way for the search. A hat blew overboard and a crewman almost followed. He was caught by those standing nearby and pulled back aboard.

Finally a cry of success came, then a wave of relieved laughter. A coconut, the last of those piled aboard at Ettal, had become wedged tight against the open steering chain.

It was yanked loose, and after a brief detour to rescue the lost hat, we were once again safely under way.

The story of that errant coconut was told many times during the following months. Each time it grew in excitement and tension. My Peace Corps experience taught me that the world is full of stories. Good or bad, sad or happy, everyone everywhere has tales to tell. The people of Chuuk tell some of the best.

Carol Severance *(Federated States of Micronesia 1966-1968) is the author of* Reefsong, *a science fiction novel describing a possible future for Pacific Islanders, based in part on her Peace Corps experience.* Reefsong *received the 1992 Compton Crook Award for best first novel. She is also the author of* Demon Drums, Storm Caller, *and* Sorcerous Sea, *a Pacific-oriented fantasy trilogy. She resides in Hilo, Hawaii, with her husband, former Chuuk Volunteer Craig J. Severance.*

Twice in My Life

by Maureen Orth

My Medellín has never been like the headlines that have been flashing around the world for a decade. The gentle "city of eternal spring," the capital of the department of Antioquia, that I lived in and cherished for two years in the sixties as a Peace Corps Volunteer has been morphed into a violent and bloodthirsty symbol of illicit drug dealing—where bombs and kidnappings have replaced conservative Catholicism and the Antiquenos' long-held reputation for entrepreneurial fervor.

Today the rap on Medellín is horrendous: The U.S. State Department warns Americans that all of Antioquia is off limits for safe travel. Journalists are especially susceptible to guerrilla attack. My Colombian *novio* of long ago, who had become a senator, was murdered in 1989 when he refused to give in to a self-styled militia leader who wanted a piece of his land. Amid this turmoil, I could only dream of going back to Medellín to visit my Peace Corps site and to see the school that I had helped build.

My memories, of course, were vivid. One Sunday a dramatic posse of five men on horseback dressed in black gaucho hats and traditional wool *ruanas* galloped up to my door in the barrio. They were leading an extra horse for me. We rode straight up into the mountains for about three miles to meet an isolated community of *campesinos* in a *vereda* called Aguas Frias. The people were desperate for a school.

Several Sundays later we began with a community work day and formed a human chain to throw rocks down the mountainside to clear the land. A year later there was a brick building that on dedication day bore a crude hand-lettered sign that was a happy surprise to me: *Escuela Marina Orth*.

I had not seen that school since 1979. Then suddenly an invitation came out of the blue from Friends of Colombia, our in-country group, and I thought that I must go. In the fall of 1995 I became part of an official goodwill tour of Colombia, one of a dozen former Colombia Peace Corps Volunteers graciously invited by the Colombian ambassador to visit four cities. Medellín was not on the itinerary, but I could easily go there by myself. Things had calmed down, I was told, since the world's most notorious *narcotraficante*, Pablo Escobar, had been killed.

Then a curious thing happened: I became afraid of the depth of my own emotions. I couldn't even think of going back to Medellín without choking up inside. So many intense memories of specific people and the majestic, sweeping Andean countryside came flooding back—not to mention the Spanish language, the music, the freedom of galloping on a horse through grass as high as my shoulders.

Of course in those days we called the rain forest the jungle; there were families of fifteen and twenty children, and good girls still courted through grilled windows; the young man wasn't allowed inside until he had declared. What if what I now saw broke my heart? We all knew the culture minutely; we had such a strong sense of identification with a country completely different from our own, and I was so young then, yet, never afraid of anything—not of living alone in a barrio considered rough, not of the rigid power structure that I believed kept my poverty-stricken neighbors locked in a dead-end destiny, and certainly not of the Peace Corps rules and regulations. The arrogance of youth—just leave us alone to do our work.

About a month before I was due to arrive, I wrote to the *señora directora* of the school at Aguas Frias and had an old friend who lived in the city deliver it for me. She could get there by jeep, my friend reported—the road was now paved and a horse was no longer required.

I didn't even recognize my old barrio, Las Violetas. Where once you had to cross a creek with water coming halfway up the bus' wheels to enter, today the creek is gone and the barrio, even more teeming with people and cars—cars!—looks not poor anymore but typical of a Colombian blue-collar neighborhood, an extension of a more prosperous area that used to be a few miles away.

As we climbed the road it was reassuring to see the towering Andes flanking us. The higher we climbed, the calmer I felt. At least the dark green mountains hadn't changed. And then we turned a curve and the day became magical. Two smiling, scrubbed little boys in brand-new uniforms were out on the road to greet me, waving paper Colombian flags.

We parked below and they ran ahead to lead me up the steep steps (another innovation) to the carved-out mountain where we had built the school. "Here she comes!" they cried. At the top of the steps, in tears and hiding her face in her skirt, was my kind neighbor from across the street in the barrio, Doña Mariela—mother of fifteen, grandmother of forty, now widowed, now living close to the school. I too began to cry as I hugged her, the first of many tears that day.

The school looked fantastic. A second story had been added, hanging pots of tropical flowers were suspended from the upper corridor, and just below on the front wall was a big metal sign donated by a local soft drink company that said "Escuela Marina Orth." Next to it hung a second hand-lettered sign: "Welcome Home." Instead of the 35 students in two classrooms that I knew of in the sixties, there were now 120 children in grades one through five. I was amazed and unprepared for the six-hour homage to come.

Slowly and shyly, men and women I had known and worked with came from around corners and behind pillars to greet me. They brought me lemons from their gardens. They told me of births and deaths and invited me to their houses. I was most thrilled to hear that some children from the school had gone on to the university and were now professionals working in Medellín, a nearly inconceivable dream when we began. They exclaimed at and eagerly grabbed pictures of my family that I had brought to show them.

Then I saw Luis Eduardo, the humble, soft-spoken president of the *vereda's* community action *junta* and really the co-founder of the school as well. A portrait of us taken together nearly thirty years ago, now tattered, was brought out for our inspection. How many times Luis Eduardo and I had ridden to town together to knock on doors in the city government to beg for bricks and mortar. He was so quietly persistent that he had been hired by the city of Medellín to work in its office of school construction, a big step up for his family.

The children, shined up bright, were taking their places outside to raise the flag and sing for me the Colombian and Antiquenan anthems. The principal presented me with a beautiful homegrown arrangement of orchids, lilies, and roses, and gave me a formal speech of introduction. With the children standing at attention, she announced a twelve-act program in my honor to be followed by a lunch, a serenade, a toast, and a mass!

I was standing but I felt I should sit. The moment was surreal. It seemed that I could almost touch the other side of the mountain. The populous valley of Medellín was spread out below, and I was surrounded by these beautiful children honoring me in a school that bore my name. Was I really in this exotic place on this cool, sunny Friday morning so far away from the rest of my life? I missed my family and wished they could share this with me. Nevertheless, I felt completely at home.

At the end, mass in this setting was simple and moving, celebrated by a young priest in white vestments on a makeshift outdoor altar in front of the school.

The mass to me was the most important part of the day. The people's faith remains strong and as a Catholic myself I felt a special bond in sharing it with them, in having the children come up to touch my hand to wish me peace, and to take Communion with them.

I tried to make my fifth speech of thanks and told the congregation that the whole idea of the Peace Corps was to plant the seed so that the community could go on as they had. This was my real thanks—that they had persevered. As I turned to go I realized that at least once in my life, when I was young, enthusiastic, and just doing my job, I actually accomplished something that my country and my family could be proud of. And twice in my life, the Peace Corps and the people of Colombia had given me more than I could have ever imagined.

Maureen Orth *(Colombia 1964-1966) is a special correspondent for* Vanity Fair. *Orth has also written for* Newsweek *and* New York *magazines, the* New York Times, Vogue, *and* Rolling Stone. *She is the author of* Vulgar Favors: Andrew Cunanan, Gianni Versace and the Largest Failed Manhunt in U.S. History. *She earned a B.A. in political science from the University of California, Berkeley, and holds an M.A. in documentary film and journalism from the University of California, Los Angeles.*

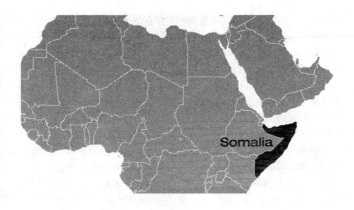

Somalia

Finding My Village
by Ambassador Charles R. Baquet III

"Are you crazy?" asked my father. "After all we sacrificed to put you through college, you're going to Africa to work for nothing?"

It was 1965 and I had just told my family that I was quitting my job as a social studies teacher in New Orleans to become a Peace Corps Volunteer in the Somali Republic. I assured my father that my college loan would be deferred and now he could get that new truck for his electrical business. When I completed two years, the Peace Corps would give me a readjustment allowance to pave my way into graduate school and jobs.

My mother worried about my health and safety, and I assured my mother that the Peace Corps was not sending Volunteers where it wasn't safe. My assurances didn't soothe my Catholic grandmother. She feared for my salvation in a far-off Muslim country. "Will you promise me you will go to mass every Sunday?"

"Yes," I lied, sinning to relieve her anxiety.

I probably wouldn't have persisted if I hadn't seen how much my cousin, Ron Ferrier, had gained from serving two years in Ethiopia. He had become one of "Kennedy's kids" in 1962, before the year-old Peace Corps had proved it could accomplish its three-part mission: providing trained Americans to help developing countries, promoting a better understanding of Americans in those countries, and giving Americans a better understanding of other people.

Besides, at twenty-five, I was restless. I longed to see the people and places I had read about in mission magazines as a child. I was in turmoil over the civil rights movement's conflicting methods, which ranged from the Rev. Martin Luther King's advocacy of nonviolence to the Black Panthers' urban activism. I wanted distance to gain perspective.

And I did. My two years as a Peace Corps Volunteer helped me find my focus and led me to an exciting, satisfying career as a Foreign Service officer, an ambassador, and—completing the circle—the Deputy Director of the Peace Corps.

Nowadays when I urge African Americans to contribute two years of their energy and abilities, I tell them from firsthand knowledge that they will receive more than they give. Hundreds of the 165,000 Americans who have joined the Peace Corps since 1961 have told me this. They say it no matter where they served, and whether they volunteered in the idealistic 1960s, the cynical 1970s, the materialistic 1980s, or the rejuvenated 1990s.

My own life illustrates the point. My two-year assignment was to teach English and social studies at a boys' school in Erigavo, a village in northern Somalia. The British had built the school during their seventy-five-year colonial rule, and English was the language of instruction.

Soon after I arrived, a Somali asked me why I had come. "I am a black American and I came to find my village," I told him, proud of my profundity.

He laughed. "You're a fool. You have come all this way to find a village that doesn't exist. After 300 years, you are a different people than we are. There's a village for you someplace. Find that place of peace in your heart and soul. There you will find your village."

I was devastated. I knew he was right. I had to turn within to find my village. His insight accelerated my search.

Teaching with few materials and living with no conveniences left little time for introspection. I shared half of a metal-roofed cement duplex with two other Volunteers, John Schecter from Wisconsin and Rozier Martin from Maine. They taught science and math, and the three of us ran the school. We had little in common except that we had all attended Catholic schools, but we became close friends.

They helped me ease my grandmother's fears. When we made the two-day trek to the nearest town, we found a priest but no Catholic church. He posed with me by a mosque that, at the right camera angle, looked like a church. I mailed the photos to my grandmother. Later, on leave in Kenya, I posed for photos with a man in dark robes in front of an Indian temple.

I knew those photos would comfort her more than hearing that the Somalis were ascetic, devout Sufi Muslims whose spirituality I admired.

Their diet of camel's milk, goat meat, and rice, however, soon sent me to the cookbook in the foot locker provided for each Volunteer household. I learned to cook goat meatloaf and lasagna outdoors on our charcoal brazier.

We missed vegetables. Forewarned by my cousin, I had brought a trunk stuffed with things I might need, including garden seeds. The Peace Corps tradition demands that you do more than your job, so growing vegetables became a special project. All went well until we left home for a few days. We returned to find goats had destroyed our sprouts. We suspected sabotage.

Another special project was stocking a library with books from discarded Peace Corps book lockers. When I went on vacation, the books disappeared. Students claimed ignorance.

Still another effort was providing recreation. My trunk held rope for making a volleyball net. We three Volunteers spent many hours figuring out the proper pattern and wove the net. The next time we were gone, the volleyball net vanished. Students said nomads had taken it.

When I completed my two years, I questioned whether I had really helped my students. In fact, until 1991, my Peace Corps experience seemed incomplete because all my special projects had failed. Yet I felt good about having managed a school and having been creative in solving problems. I came back feeling I could do anything.

Two weeks after I arrived in the United States, I was a program officer for VISTA, the domestic version of the Peace Corps. The Director was R. Sargent Shriver, the irrepressibly optimistic brother-in-law of President John F. Kennedy, who had chosen him to be the first Director of the Peace Corps.

In 1968, I started looking for a job in international development. President Lyndon Johnson urged the State Department to recruit minorities as career Foreign Service officers. Thanks to recommendations from embassy staff I had met in Somalia and from the Peace Corps, I became part of the first minority group to train for the Foreign Service under the president's executive order. My first assignment was the U.S. Embassy in Paris. I've also served in Hong Kong, Beirut, Cape Town, Djibouti, and Washington, D.C. My assignments included a year at Syracuse University, where I earned a master's degree, and a year in the Foreign Service Senior Seminar.

As consul general in Cape Town from 1988 to 1991, I witnessed the end of apartheid in South Africa and the beginning of its constitutional process. I met the newly released Nelson Mandela and many other remarkable people. I also saw the great contrasts between the cities and the countryside. I would not have hesitated, for example, to have open-heart surgery in Cape Town, but in rural areas I feared a cut.

Just when I thought my career couldn't be more fulfilling, President George Bush appointed me ambassador to Djibouti, a tiny former French colony in East Africa just northwest of my Peace Corps country. I felt I was going home. But this time, tribal warfare, drought, and famine plagued the area.

Word that a returned Peace Corps Volunteer had come back as ambassador spread quickly. Northern Somalis lined up outside my office, expecting "their" ambassador to perform miracles. The elders invited me back to

Erigavo to assist with a peace and reconciliation conference of five tribes. The participants included some of my former students.

"We knew you of all people would be able to bring this reconciliation effort off," one said, and then he told me how he and other students had destroyed my garden, my library, and my volleyball net to see my reaction and what else I would pull from my trunk. I realized that even though my projects had not been successful, my work had left a lasting impression on my students. They realized as students that I had been there to help. They understood as adults that my efforts had brought them some measure of hope. At last, I thought, I had been a successful Volunteer after all.

But my connection to the Peace Corps would continue even after my time as ambassador to Djibouti. After he was elected in 1993, President Clinton nominated me to become Deputy Director of the Peace Corps. I hadn't sought the appointment, but I accepted immediately and with great enthusiasm. Beginning in January 1994, in addition to representing the Peace Corps publicly, I spent much of my time recruiting the next generation of Volunteers from America's minority communities. I believe that the Peace Corps can fulfill its mission completely only if our Volunteers reflect the rich diversity of our nation. Today, about fifteen percent of Peace Corps Volunteers are minorities, and we hope to encourage more African Americans, Hispanic Americans, Native Americans and members of other minority communities to become a part of the Peace Corps experience.

I was also fortunate to help establish the first Peace Corps project in South Africa. I led an assessment team that worked with eleven South African ministries and the president's office to create a program that would help meet the country's development needs. In February 1997, the first group of thirty-two Volunteers, ranging in age from twenty-two to sixty, arrived to begin training to address one of South Africa's greatest needs: primary education. Some rural schools don't own a single book, and their pupils bring chairs from home or sit on the floor.

The first Volunteers—sixty percent of whom were African, Asian, or Hispanic Americans—worked with teachers to develop teaching materials. After school, they helped their communities build their capacity to provide such critical elements as clean water and basic health care. Combining education and community development is tough, and we chose those first Volunteers carefully.

One was Norma Harley, age sixty, who had just returned from teaching as a Peace Corps Volunteer in Nepal. She rejected her daughter's suggestion of settling down in Sacramento and baby-sitting her grandchild. Harley told a reporter, "I've been optimistic in a lot of things that have happened in our country, coming through Martin Luther King's era and Malcolm X, and then let down in so many ways. And I really hope, in South Africa, that they don't have to go through the disappointments."

Another was C.D. Glin, age twenty-five, who put a Foreign Service opportunity on hold in order to become a Peace Corps Volunteer. He wrote anti-apartheid rap songs as a youngster and shook President Mandela's hand while attending Howard University in Washington, D.C. He was a leader of groups such as Concerned Black Men, a mentoring organization. He also tutored immigrants in English.

South Africa is a country that is rich in both natural and human resources. As always, the Peace Corps strives to work itself out of a job, which it has done now in more than thirty countries. If all goes well, the country will require Peace Corps assistance for no more than ten years.

Another program I am especially interested in is Haiti. My father's family came from Haiti to Louisiana in 1809, and my mother's family just before 1900. Haiti was the slave ships' last stop before the United States, and the place and people have the look of Africa. They are warm, hospitable, and hard working, and many of them are incredibly poor.

The Peace Corps program in Haiti was suspended in 1991 because of a military coup. But in 1996—after U.S. forces had helped restore democracy—Peace Corps Volunteers returned. That year I went to Haiti to swear in a new group of Volunteers and visit the first group. Most were working with farm cooperatives to improve mango, avocado, and papaya trees so that Haitians can raise commercially acceptable varieties to market abroad. Like modern Johnny Appleseeds, the Volunteers are grafting imported varieties onto the disease-resistant local trees. For example, Haitian-born Solange Lee, age fifty-eight, holds a master's degree in rehabilitation counseling from Hunter College and was the supervisor of a shelter for the homeless in Brooklyn. Christine Steinmann, a veterinarian in Arizona, had worked in Kenya. She is developing an animal husbandry program.

In each of these Volunteers and hundreds of others whom I visited around the world, I see the same sense of adventure, interest in other cultures, and desire to do something meaningful that I felt when I served as a

Volunteer in the 1960s. This is the great genius of the Peace Corps—Americans serving our country by making a difference in the lives of other people. And just as I did when I found my village in Somalia, the men and women who are serving in the Peace Corps are laying the foundations for their future lives by finding their own inner villages now.

Charles R. Baquet III *(Somalia 1965-1967) taught English and social studies at the Dayaha School in Erigavo and at the Hargeisa Girls School and Hargeisa Technical School in Hargeisa. Baquet received a B.A. in history and English literature from Xavier University of Louisiana, and earned his M.A. in public administration from the Maxwell School of Government at Syracuse University. He has been a Foreign Service officer for 35 years, posted in Paris, Hong Kong, Beirut, and Cape Town (as consul general), and served as ambassador to Djibouti (1991-93) before his appointment as Deputy Director of the Peace Corps. He is currently the director of the Center for Intercultural and International Programs at Xavier University of Louisiana.*

The Vision

by Sargent Shriver

Oscar Wilde is said to have observed that America really was discovered by a dozen people before Columbus but that the discovery remained a secret. I am tempted to feel that way about the Peace Corps. A national effort of this type had been proposed many times in previous years, but only in 1961 did it become reality.

In quantitative terms, the Peace Corps has never been a big idea. It started in the first year with a few thousand Americans being dispatched to serve in the underdeveloped world, and though the number has gone up and down, the concept has remained essentially the same. Compared with the millions in uniform who have served America abroad, the ambition was modest—perhaps too modest. Compared with the funds our government transmits in foreign aid to countries less affluent than ours, the budget was barely visible. Still, those of us who were present at the creation nurtured the notion that the Peace Corps had a huge potential for promoting the peace of the world and the well-being of humanity. After forty years, though poverty and war remain with us, I think I see some evidence that we were right. Qualitatively, the Peace Corps has succeeded.

My own interest in the Peace Corps idea had started quite a few years before, when I was a part of and, later, leader for Experiment in International Living groups in Europe in the 1930s. In the 1950s I visited several Asian countries—Japan, Korea, Vietnam, Cambodia, Thailand—and, when I returned, I proposed sending three-man political action teams to Asia, Africa, and Latin America. These teams were to consist of vigorous and imaginative young labor leaders, businessmen, and politicians. They would offer their services at a grass-roots level and work directly with the people, contributing to the growth of the economies, to the democratic organization of the societies, and to the peaceful outcome of the social revolutions under way. When the idea of the Peace Corps emerged during the presidential campaign of 1960, it seemed to offer the possibility of realizing, in a new form, this old objective, which seemed to me more important than ever.

A month or so after President Kennedy took office, he asked me to report to him on how the Peace Corps could be organized, and then to organize it. John Kennedy believed Americans had decent ideals that were going untapped, and a physical and spiritual resilience that was being unused. He told me to make the Peace Corps a tough agency, to prove wrong those who were skeptical about the willingness of Americans, especially young Americans, to make the kinds of sacrifices that the Peace Corps would require. "Go ahead," he said, "you can do it," and to do it we assembled the best people we could find from the professions, from our universities and foundations, from our corporations and unions, from private agencies and civil service. We knew the Peace Corps would have only one chance to work. We felt like parachute jumpers: The chute had to open the first time, or we were sure to come to an abrupt end.

Within the team I had assembled, we wrestled with a hundred questions of policy, debating around the clock, in those early days of 1961. Not the least of the questions was the name we would give to the undertaking. For a while,

"Peace Corps," which Kennedy had used during the election campaign, was not the first choice. Some of the president's advisors scoffed at it, arguing for a solid bureaucratic title like "Agency for Overseas Voluntary Service." Conservatives, furthermore, said the word "peace" sounded soft, vague, and weak. They insisted communists had corrupted it by applying it to every political initiative and even to every war they were involved in. Not to be outdone, many liberals disliked the word "corps." They said it sounded militaristic.

But I thought we should try to recapture the term "peace," to liberate it, so to speak. I thought we should be able to use it without it sounding like propaganda, metaphor, or corn. As for "corps," I was not uncomfortable with conveying the militance of our purpose, at least a quiet militance. The fact was that I could not visualize the elimination of war except through the kind of effort in which the Peace Corps was to engage. Peace was our goal, and we were not embarrassed to envisage this effort as a genuine way station along the road.

Our Peace Corps task force worked literally day and night for weeks, readying recommendations for the president. John Kennedy had set the theme of the new administration with his inaugural statement, "Ask not what your country can do for you, ask what you can do for your country." Those were inspiring words, and at that point, many were asking, "All right, what can we do for our country?" We considered speed essential in order to maintain the momentum of the Kennedy theme.

By March 1, 1961, we were ready with a detailed report, which recommended to President Kennedy the Peace Corps' immediate, full-scale establishment. We rejected proposals for pilot programs or small, experimental initiatives. We asked for an independent agency, not answerable to the Agency for International Development, and we turned down suggestions to limit the mission of the Peace Corps to supplementing efforts of the Junior Red Cross, the Chamber of Commerce, or other American groups working abroad. We rejected uniforms, badges, medals, and any other distinctive clothing, along with rankings and grades. We said we wanted no special housing, food, schools, or anything else, except health services: We decided to send our own doctors to care for the Volunteers. We even promised to discourage vacations in the "fleshpot" cities of the world, though many were accessible.

Since 1961, the Peace Corps has sent more than 165,000 Americans to serve overseas. They are patriots, committed to the special vision upon which the Peace Corps was founded, and they have helped to disseminate this vision far and wide. As Americans in service abroad, they have gone beyond careerism, beyond fun and adventure, to dedicate their best efforts to the idea of raising up humanity.

The Peace Corps is unique among American institutions. Though it is an agency of government, it is profoundly nonpolitical. That does not mean the Peace Corps is indifferent to the national interests of the United States. But it was conceived to reach beyond domestic political goals, and beyond international rivalries, to touch the deepest hopes of man. Without trumpets, banners, or weapons, the Peace Corps serves America abroad. It renders this service to our country by promoting an idea of an America that is caring and humane.

I suspect the reason so few people appreciate our ideas and ideals is that we ourselves fail to understand our potential in this area. As a result, we consistently sell ourselves short. When we hear of a "secret" American power, our minds seem to turn automatically to killer devices. It is true that our weapons and our wealth are what are most clearly visible to the majority of the world. But our real "secret" power, I believe, is the vitality of our democratic life. I would like to quote David Crozier, who lost his life in an air accident while serving as a Peace Corps Volunteer in Colombia. In a sadly prophetic letter to his parents, he said, "Should it come to it, I would rather give my life trying to help someone than to give my life looking down a gun barrel at him."

But let me assert the Peace Corps is no naïve organization, aiming to do good while indifferent to the existence of evil in the world. We know the United States is involved in a contest of ideologies being waged in many arenas, not the least of them the underdeveloped nations. The Peace Corps plays a role in this struggle. But let us be clear that its role lies not in its solicitation of these nations' support for America's political positions, much less our alliances. The role lies in the contribution the Peace Corps makes to their success. If these countries succeed in their plans for economic, social, and political progress, it will not matter much whether they agree with us on a given issue, or even whether they like us. If they become healthy, democratic societies, they will not be a threat to world peace. This is what matters.

The arena in which the Peace Corps makes its stand for America is in the nations where a peaceful outcome to the world's ideological struggle remains possible. Most of the African continent meets that test, as do Latin America and East Asia. But I exclude no region of the world. Though the

Peace Corps Volunteers carry no rifles to battle, they serve their country on fronts that are vital to the peace of the world. They serve in the developing world, home for hundreds of millions of people whose only ideology is to create a decent life for themselves, a life that measures richness with dignity, that is free of fear and instability. The time to reach them is not when military action becomes necessary, when war or violent revolution is impending. Peace Corps Volunteers are not trained to deal with enemies bearing arms. Their enemies are hunger, ignorance, and disease. By forcing these enemies into retreat, the Peace Corps serves humanity's interests, and America's.

It seems a paradox to say that Peace Corps Volunteers make their contribution to American foreign policy by staying out of the foreign policy establishment, but it is true. Peace Corps Volunteers are not trained diplomats, not propagandists. For the most part, they are not even technical experts. They represent our society by what they are, what they do, and the spirit in which they do it. They scrupulously steer clear of intelligence activities and local politics. The Peace Corps' strict adherence to these principles has been a crucial factor in the decision of politically uncommitted countries to invite American Volunteers into their homes, and even into their classrooms to teach future generations of national leadership. In an era of sabotage and espionage, Peace Corps Volunteers have earned a priceless but simple renown: They are trustworthy.

When the Peace Corps goes abroad, it spreads the ideal of a free and democratic society. Its strategic premise is the sense of concern that every member has shown by the act of volunteering. The Peace Corps' secret weapon is example. This example proclaims that in America, the color of a Volunteer's skin, or a human's religious or political beliefs, do not determine personal dignity and worth. We have sent black Americans to white men's countries, white Americans to black men's countries. We were told that we could not send Protestants to certain parts of Catholic countries in Latin America, and that we could not send Jews to Arab countries. But we sent them. Rarely have these decisions spawned discontent. Far more often, they have elicited admiration and, if I may say so, even envy. On a practical level, what a Volunteer has left behind may be a newly constructed well, or a proficiency among a few students in English, or a better way to raise corn. But he or she has also left behind the germ of the Peace Corps vision, and it is a germ that inevitably spreads. I believe there are few more important contributions to be made.

We never meant for Peace Corps Volunteers to go abroad as promoters of a particular political theory or economic system, much less a religious creed. But that did not mean they were without a mission. The Volunteer goes overseas as a willing and skilled worker. He or she also goes as a representative of the ideals that America, with all its imperfections, embodies better than any society in our time. It is the idea that free and committed men and women can cross, even transcend, boundaries of culture and language, of foreign tradition, and great disparities of wealth and culture, to work in harmony with one another. The Peace Corps has a commitment to overcome old hostilities and entrenched nationalisms, to bring knowledge where ignorance has dominated, to challenge traditions that may enslave, even as it respects the societies from which they emerge. The Peace Corps was designed for different cultures to meet on the common ground of service to human welfare and personal worth so that men and women might share what is valuable in the spirit of each.

Those of us who were around at the beginning conspired in sending Volunteers off on assignment as free men and women. I say "conspired" because what they secretly carried in their baggage, along with the books and clean socks, was the Peace Corps idea. As Americans, they were free to travel, to write, to read, and to speak as they chose. They were surrounded by no wall of censorship, nor constrained by any authoritarian code of discipline. They were trained to work with people, and not to employ them or give them orders. Volunteers from the start were instructed to do what the country in which they served wanted them to do, not what they, out of some sense of cultural superiority, thought was best for their hosts. That does not mean Volunteers did not often have to rely on their own initiative to make best use of their time and talent. The Peace Corps encouraged their initiative. The staff provided the framework and then relied on the creative energies of dedicated individuals to fill in the spaces.

For forty years the Peace Corps has remained faithful to this vision. Very early, the Peace Corps perceived the trap of neocolonialism, and Volunteers understood that they must, if necessary, go out of their way to avoid it. They have lived not in some figurative house on the hill, not in isolated compounds or chic neighborhoods, but physically among the people they have served, in intimate contact with them. A visiting Ghanaian once said to me, "Peace Corps teachers in my country don't live so badly. After all, they live as well as we do." We did not inflict discomfort on the Volunteer for discomfort's sake. Rather, by their way of life Volunteers have shown that material privilege has not become the central and indispensable ingredient in American life.

From the beginning, Peace Corps Volunteers have not only lived sparely but eaten the food and talked the language of rural villagers, of dwellers of the barrios, of communities of seaside fishermen. They shopped for bargains in the marketplace and rode in buses or on bicycles. They enjoyed no diplomatic immunity and observed the same local laws as everyone else. They received modest living allowances in the field, sums fixed to match local conditions, far from conventional American salaries. They sweated in hot climates without air conditioning and made their own fires in wood stoves when the weather was cold.

Living in the developing world, Peace Corps Volunteers have learned new facts of life. They have escaped from what is all too often a kind of cultural imprisonment, brought on by American affluence, and exposed themselves to the reality of life in much of the world. This is a world that, for all of its richness of culture, often still lives on the edge of survival. I could feel the suffering of the Peace Corps Volunteer who wrote to me from East Africa, "People die here for want of so little." How many Americans have the painful privilege of learning that lesson?

The Volunteers who brought back from their experience abroad a revised sense of the human condition also acquired an appreciation of the fact that answers to its problems are generally much more complex than they appear at first glance. Those who think there are panaceas for the ills of emerging nations, who believe all that is needed is more money or more schools or a few more dams, or even more democracy or more private enterprise, never served in the Peace Corps. The wisdom that Volunteers brought back with them has added to the reservoir of compassion and understanding in America. It has provided our nation with insight into the thinking of the great majority with whom we share the globe. But Peace Corps Volunteers, because they were toilers and not just observers, also learned that they need not sit by impotently while others suffer. That, too, is an important lesson for America.

So, in 2001, we look back across forty years of soul-filled history. We have known the summer heat of the Sahara, the biting cold of the Alte Plano of Peru, the endless rain of the Asian monsoons. We have often overcome the obstacles of the federal bureaucracy, only to stumble over our own mistakes. But we have survived, and precious gifts have been bestowed upon us. We have seen the smile on the face of a child whom a Volunteer has taught to read. We have been grateful that a Volunteer has had a hand in building a feeder road, establishing a credit union, forming a cooperative for buying a tractor or marketing fish. We have marveled at the energy of a people in a dusty village after a Volunteer has persuaded them to lift the dead hand of hopelessness.

In forty years, the Peace Corps has made a start. The idea is in the air, a seed being carried on the breeze of human contact to people and institutions throughout the world. I do not know how many converts the Peace Corps has made, but I would like to think it has dealt a solid blow to ignorance and hunger. I want to believe it has moved human dignity to a higher plane. I pray it has moved peace a trifle closer, while chasing the shadow of nuclear war to a more distant reach.

Regretfully, I acknowledge it will require more time and still greater effort for the vision of the Peace Corps to win the world. That a pugnacious nationalism seems once again to be sweeping over our country does not so much mean that the Peace Corps has failed as that it has not tried hard enough. I know that, even in its brief life, the Peace Corps has emitted a glow, faint though it may be, that has helped light the way to a better and more peaceful life over a great area of the Earth's surface. I take its triumphs, however, not as a cause for congratulation, but as a challenge. After forty years, the task ahead is clear: to bring the Peace Corps and its ideals back to the top of America's agenda.

Sargent Shriver *(Peace Corps Director 1961-1966) founded the Peace Corps under President Kennedy. Following his five years with the agency, he was the first director of the Office of Economic Opportunity, which created VISTA, Head Start, and Job Corps among other anti-poverty programs. Later he served as U.S. ambassador to France in the Johnson administration. A graduate of Yale University and Yale Law School, Shriver served in the U.S. Navy for five years. In 1994 he was presented with the Medal of Freedom by President Clinton. He is now the chairman of the board of Special Olympics International.*

I Stand in Awe

by Loret Miller Ruppe

Loret Miller Ruppe was appointed the eleventh Director of the Peace Corps by President Ronald Reagan in 1981. During her distinguished eight-year tenure, Director Ruppe strengthened the Peace Corps in immeasurable ways, carried out an expansive vision of its role in the world, and provided strong support to Peace Corps Volunteers. She left the Peace Corps in 1989 as the longest-serving Director in the agency's history.

The following remarks are taken from her address at the Peace Corps' thirty-fifth anniversary celebration in Washington, D.C., on March 1, 1996.—Editors

In 1983, I was invited to the White House for the state visit of Prime Minister Ratu Mara of Fiji. Everyone took their seats around an enormous table—President Reagan, Vice President Bush, Caspar Weinberger, the rest of the Cabinet, with the prime minister and his delegation, and myself. They talked about world conditions, sugar quotas, nuclear-free zones. The president asked the prime minister to make his presentation. A very distinguished gentleman, he drew himself up and said, "President Reagan, I bring you today the sincere thanks of my government and my people." Everyone held their breath and there was total silence. "For the men and women of the Peace Corps who go out into our villages, who live with our people." He went on and on. I beamed. Vice President Bush leaned over afterward and whispered, "What did you pay that man to say that?"

A week later, the Office of Management and Budget presented the budget to President Reagan with a cut for the Peace Corps. President Reagan said, "Don't cut the Peace Corps. It's the only thing I got thanked for last week at the state dinner." The Peace Corps' budget went up. Vice President Bush asked kiddingly again, "What did you pay?"

Well, we know one thing: It isn't for pay that Volunteers give their blood, their sacred honor. I can never forget the sweat, the tears, the frustrations, the best efforts and successes of thousands of Peace Corps Volunteers. I stand in awe and with the deepest respect. I always thought I could be a Volunteer until I went out and met them.

I ended many speeches when I was Peace Corps Director with this: Peace, that beautiful five-letter word we all say we crave and pray for, is up for grabs in the '90s. A question must be answered above and beyond this special forum: Is peace simply the absence of war? Or is it the absence of the conditions that bring on war, the conditions of hunger, disease, poverty, illiteracy, and despair?

When fifty percent of the children die in a village before they are five, when women walk miles for water and then search for wood to cook by, when farmers leave their villages where there are no jobs to flock to cities where there are no jobs, when neighbors ethnically cleanse their neighbors, then let's face it, America, the world is not at peace.

And here at home, when fifty percent of our children live below the poverty level in many of our cities, when the homeless abound on our streets, when our nation's capital is bankrupt and our schools require metal detectors, racial tensions abound and immigrant bashing and downsizing terrorize loyal workers, then let's face it, America, we are not at peace.

The Peace Corps family must respond again to "Ask not what your country can do for you, rather ask what you can do for your country." And today, in our world, it is, as President Kennedy said, the "towering task." We can do it!

Loret Miller Ruppe *received the Shriver Award for her outstanding work as Peace Corps Director from 1981 to 1989. She died in 1996.*

How to Become a Peace Corps Volunteer

There's a Place for You in the Peace Corps

If you have a college degree, a sense of adventure, and the desire to help other people help themselves, a Peace Corps recruiter wants to talk with you. Most Peace Corps Volunteers are college graduates with degrees in liberal arts, such as history, political science, English, social studies, information technology/computer science, or psychology. The Peace Corps can find assignments for people with degrees in photography, theater, and other fine arts. There is also a need for people with degrees in non-liberal arts fields, such as business, engineering, and the sciences. In addition, there are opportunities for individuals with professional skills and work experience (in such areas as business, technical trades, and agriculture) and a commitment to service, but who may not have a college degree.

People with liberal arts degrees often have a well-rounded education and a perspective that brings creativity and versatility to their Volunteer assignments. You may have gained experience from specialized academic or vocational courses, summer jobs, hobbies, or other interests that can make you a strong candidate for service as a Volunteer and help the Peace Corps find a place for you overseas. Computer skills and previous work as a counselor, as a volunteer in your community, or as an assistant in a classroom setting are the kinds of experiences that are needed in all countries where the Peace Corps has programs. And, if necessary, your Peace Corps recruiter can suggest a range of activities that you can undertake now to help sharpen your skills for a Volunteer assignment.

The Facts: Benefits

Two Years of Service— a Lifetime of Benefits

It is important to join the Peace Corps for the right reasons: a sincere desire to help, to make a difference, to change something for the better. But it's also important to know that for all the giving Peace Corps Volunteers do, they also receive a great deal in return. From practical benefits such as student loan deferment to career benefits like fluency in a foreign language to the intangible benefits that come with making a difference in people's lives, there are a variety of rewards Volunteers receive for their dedicated service,—rewards that will last a lifetime.

Career Benefits

The skills that are required of a successful Volunteer are those required in just about any career. The Peace Corps allows individuals an opportunity to develop and strengthen these skills in another country and a different culture.

From government to business to education, returned Volunteers have used their Peace Corps experience as a foundation for successful careers in a variety of areas. Priscilla Wrubel, returned Volunteer and founder of the Nature Company, says, "It's the Peace Corps experience that allowed us to start something as crazy as the Nature Company."

Former Chrysler Corporation Chairman Lee Iacocca stated, "The continued growth of America is going to depend more and more upon the kinds of skills, perspectives, and cross-cultural experiences brought back by returning Peace Corps Volunteers."

In the global marketplace of today's business world, the overseas experience, cross-cultural knowledge, and language skills that Volunteers develop are extremely valuable and highly sought after. The Peace Corps' Office of Returned Volunteer Services publishes a newsletter that features many companies that are seeking the skills of returned Volunteers and provides career counseling services. Furthermore, one's status as a returned Volunteer provides an advantage in applying for certain government jobs.

Educational Benefits

The Peace Corps experience is in itself an education, but there are many other benefits that relate to a Volunteer's previous or future education. Volunteers can defer payments on many student loans. In the case of Perkins Loans, a percentage of the principal and interest may be canceled for each year of Peace Corps service.

In some instances, academic credit is granted for Peace Corps service and training, which may also satisfy field-work or practicum requirements. More than fifty colleges and universities offer scholarships and assistantships for returned Peace Corps Volunteers.

Often, individuals find themselves struggling to decide between attending graduate school and joining the Peace Corps. For many of these individuals, the Master's International Program combines the best of both worlds. It offers the unique opportunity to combine Peace Corps service with a master's degree program. For Peace Corps Volunteers who wish to pursue an education back at home post-service, the Peace Corps also sponsors the Fellows/USA Program, which provides eligible individuals with tuition assistance and scholarships for advanced degree programs at participating colleges and universities nationwide.

Financial Benefits

Of course, there are so many more benefits to the Peace Corps than money, but Volunteers' financial needs are not ignored. Volunteers receive a monthly living allowance that enables them to live in a manner similar to others in their community. Medical and dental care is provided, as is transportation to and from the country of service. Volunteers also receive twenty-four vacation days per year. Finally, after the completion of three months of training and two years of service, Volunteers receive $6,075 to help them readjust and begin life after their overseas assignment.

The benefits of Peace Corps service do not end with one's service. The experience is something that affects Volunteers' lives long after they return home. It is an experience they draw upon for the rest of their lives and as they become members of the larger community of returned Volunteers across the country. As is often said, the Peace Corps isn't simply something great. It's the beginning of something great.

Support Is Never Far Away

Volunteers Make the Difference

The Peace Corps is only as effective as its Volunteers. Moreover, Volunteers can only be effective if they are safe, healthy, and properly trained. That's why, over the years, the Peace Corps has developed an extensive training and support program to ensure the well-being of Volunteers.

Pre-service Training

To prepare for their job assignments, Peace Corps Volunteers participate in a three-month training program in the country where they will serve. While in training, they often live with a host family. Volunteers receive intensive instruction in the local language, most often from native speakers. Volunteers learn the technical skills necessary for their assignments and receive extensive information about the local culture and traditions. At the completion of the training program, Volunteers are sent to their designated sites with the language, technical, and cross-cultural skills they will need to begin their assignments.

Health and Safety Support

The health and safety of every Volunteer is the Peace Corps' highest priority. The Peace Corps devotes significant resources to promote the health and safety of Volunteers and to provide them with the training, support, and information necessary for a healthy and safe volunteer experience. When establishing a program, the Peace Corps considers the health and safety circumstances in each country where Volunteers serve. Volunteers are assigned to areas that are chosen according to specific safety criteria that consider housing, transportation, communication, access to services, and proximity to fellow Volunteers. In addition, every Volunteer receives training on health and safety issues relevant to the area in which he or she is serving.

In every country where Volunteers serve, the Peace Corps has a basic medical unit and medical provider. They brief Volunteers on staying healthy and provide them with the basic medical skills and supplies needed to do so. If a health problem occurs that cannot be treated locally, the Peace Corps will send the Volunteer to an appropriate facility in a nearby country or back to the United States. All requisite vaccinations are given before and during a Volunteer's service. This health and safety support system continues throughout every Volunteer's service.

Because Peace Corps Volunteers serve in some of the least developed countries and in some of the most remote areas in the world, health, safety, and security risks are an inherent part of life and of Volunteer service. The Peace Corps expects Volunteers to take responsibility for their personal health and safety by exercising mature, appropriate behavior and sound judgment.

In-country Support Programs

To ensure that all Volunteers can be effective throughout their service, the Peace Corps regularly provides training information and workshops, which reinforce existing skills and allow Volunteers to develop new skills as needed. In addition, Peace Corps staff periodically visit Volunteers at their sites during the course of their service.

Frequently Asked Questions

I hear it's very hard to get into the Peace Corps. Is that true? How competitive is it?

To become a Peace Corps Volunteer, an applicant must meet certain academic and work experience requirements. When evaluating an applicant, the Peace Corps considers the "whole person," including your life experiences, community involvement, volunteer work, motivations, and even your hobbies. In most cases, applicants with a bachelor's degree in any discipline, strong motivation, and a commitment to Peace Corps service will be competitive to become Peace Corps Volunteers.

Can I choose the country where I'll serve as a Volunteer? How long is a Peace Corps assignment?

The Peace Corps makes every effort to accommodate your interests and preferences for serving as a Volunteer, but cannot guarantee placement in any specific country or region. The main priority is to place you in a country where your skills are most needed, so you are encouraged to be flexible when offered an assignment. Peace Corps assignments are for two years plus an additional three months of training in your country of service.

I have student loans. Can they be deferred or canceled while I serve in the Peace Corps?

In general, during your service as a Volunteer, you may defer repayment of your Stafford Loans (formerly known as Guaranteed Student Loans), Perkins Loans, Federal Consolidation Loans, or Direct Loans. In addition, Volunteers with Perkins Loans receive a 15 percent cancellation of their outstanding balance for each year of their two years of service. The Peace Corps does not grant deferments, cancellations, or grace periods for government or private loans. You must obtain these directly from your lending institution. The regulations that authorize loan deferment and cancellation are sometimes complicated, but your Peace Corps recruiter can help explain the different rules that apply to each type of loan.

Do I need to speak another language to get into the Peace Corps?

The Peace Corps teaches more than 180 languages and dialects. During your pre-service training, you will receive intensive language instruction in order to prepare you for living and working in your overseas community. While some of the countries where Volunteers serve prefer people who have studied French or Spanish, it is not always a requirement.

Can married couples join the Peace Corps? Can I serve with my boyfriend or girlfriend?

Peace Corps service can be a rewarding and enriching experience for married couples. Today, about 10 percent of Peace Corps Volunteers are married. In all cases, both spouses must serve as Volunteers, while living and working in the same community. Applicants can begin the Peace Corps application process while engaged, but must be married before departing for their overseas assignment.

The Peace Corps, however, is unable to place couples with dependent children and cannot guarantee placement in the same country of couples or friends who are not legally married.

Do I have to have a specific degree to get into the Peace Corps?

About 97 percent of all Peace Corps Volunteers have a bachelor's degree. While specific environmental, business, or education degrees can be necessary in qualifying for some assignments, if you have completed a college degree and have a sincere commitment to service, your recruiter can help find an assignment that is right for you. There are also assignments for applicants with significant experience in such areas as business, technical trades, information technology/computer science, and agriculture who may not have a college degree.

Does the Peace Corps accept senior citizens?

You are never too old to serve in the Peace Corps. Volunteers must be at least 18 years old, but there is no upper age limit. The oldest Peace Corps Volunteer who ever served was 86 when he completed his service. The Peace Corps, and the countries in which Volunteers serve, welcome and value the wealth of experience that older Americans bring to their overseas assignments.

What kind of job placement assistance does the Peace Corps provide once I have completed my Volunteer service?

The Peace Corps' Returned Volunteer Services (RVS) provides career, educational, and other advice and assistance through its Career Center in Washington, D.C. RVS publishes a bimonthly job bulletin and career manuals and provides self-assessment tools to help returned Volunteers explore career options. In addition, for a period of one year after the completion of their service, returned Volunteers have noncompetitive eligibility status for appointments to U.S. government executive branch agencies. Under some limited circumstances, however, this status can be extended up to a maximum of three years after the completion of Peace Corps service.

How much will I be paid while volunteering with the Peace Corps? What expenses will I have as a Volunteer?

As a Peace Corps Volunteer, you are not paid a salary. Instead, you receive a stipend to cover your basic necessities—food, housing expenses, and local transportation. While the amount of the stipend varies from country to country, you will receive an amount that allows you to live at the same level as the people you serve in your community. However, it will be your responsibility to take care of all of your personal expenses—souvenirs and vacation travel. The Peace Corps pays for your transportation to and from your country of service and provides you with complete medical and dental care. At the conclusion of your service as a Volunteer, you will receive a "readjustment allowance" of $225 for each month of service. If you complete your full term of service, you will receive $6,075.

Do I get vacation time while I'm overseas? Can I come home for a visit? Can my family or friends visit me?

The Peace Corps provides two vacation days for every month of service completed. You may wish to travel home for a visit, or your family and friends can make the trip to visit you in your overseas community. Visiting a Peace Corps Volunteer is one of the most exciting ways to see and learn about another country's people, cultures, and traditions. The cost of your vacation travel, home or elsewhere, is your responsibility.

Will I be the only Peace Corps Volunteer in my community? Will I be in an isolated spot? Can I have a roommate?

Every Volunteer's experience is unique. Some Volunteers are placed in rural communities that are hours or even days away from the nearest Peace Corps Volunteer. Others live in bustling towns or large cities, where the nearest Volunteer lives down the street or even in the same apartment building. Serving in the Peace Corps requires flexibility and independence. So be prepared to live alone, with another Volunteer, or even with a host family.

Does my health care coverage last after my Peace Corps service overseas?
Are there any special plans I can join?

The Peace Corps offers a comprehensive health insurance package called CorpsCare, and it is specifically designed for Volunteers who have completed their service overseas, or who leave the Peace Corps for other reasons. This plan can be activated during the last month of service, and Volunteers can purchase up to eighteen months of coverage for themselves and their dependents. Volunteers are strongly urged to sign up for coverage before they leave their country of service. The Peace Corps will pay the premium for the first month, with Volunteers electing to pay for coverage thereafter. There are no preexisting-condition exclusions or other medical restrictions on eligibility for this health insurance plan.

Steps to Applying

Your Application

Make sure to fill out your application thoroughly. Once completed, submit the application, as well as the Health Status Review form, a copy of your educational transcripts, and a copy of your résumé, by mail or online to your local Peace Corps recruiting office. Your Peace Corps recruiter will be looking for detailed information about your work experience, education, volunteer experience, life skills, and hobbies.

The Peace Corps asks that you provide three references. These should be from:

- a current or previous employment supervisor;
- a volunteer work supervisor; and
- a friend.

Prior to your service, the Peace Corps' Office of Medical Services in Washington, D.C., will assess your medical and dental records. This is to ensure that you can serve safely and effectively, and that the Peace Corps' overseas medical staff will be able to handle your individual medical needs.

Your Interview

The interview with your recruiter usually takes place within a month of our receipt of your application. Most applicants are interviewed in person, though phone interviews are an option and can be arranged. During the interview, your recruiter will explore issues such as your flexibility, adaptability, social sensitivity, cultural awareness, motivation, and commitment to Peace Corps service. Working as a team, you and your recruiter will assess your skills, look at the programs available overseas, and determine if the Peace Corps is right for you. At this point, you may be required to get additional volunteer experience in order to qualify for certain programs. Once your recruiter finds an appropriate match, you may be "nominated" for a Peace Corps assignment, pending medical and legal clearances.

Medical/Dental Clearance

Your recruiting office will forward your sealed Health Status Review form to the Peace Corps Medical Office as soon as your application arrives. After you are nominated, a member of the Peace Corps' medical screening team will review your completed medical history form. Most applicants will be mailed a medical examination packet. In some instances, an applicant may be disqualified, deferred, or limited to placement in certain countries. To receive clearance, you must obtain the indicated physical and dental exams and have the forms in the packet completed. An overwhelming majority of applicants are medically qualified for Peace Corps service.

Legal Clearance

The Peace Corps has established legal standards of eligibility for all applicants. Please note that the following factors may affect your eligibility and will require clarification and documentation before you can be cleared for Peace Corps service:

- marital status;
- dependents;
- previous arrests and convictions;
- financial obligations (e.g., home mortgage payments, child support, student loans);
- bankruptcy;
- past association with U.S. intelligence activities; and
- current obligations to the military.

Finally, the Peace Corps requires information from you that will be submitted to the U.S. Federal Bureau of Investigation for a background check, along with an impression of your fingerprints.

Your Assignment

Your Peace Corps placement officer in Washington, D.C. (not your recruiter), will make the final match between the country's request for Volunteers and your skills and personal qualifications. This match is designed to ensure a successful fit for both you and a specific country's program.

Once you are invited to join the Peace Corps, an invitation packet will be mailed to you. The packet includes a Volunteer Assignment Description, passport and visa applications, and a booklet to guide you in preparing for departure.

After you have accepted an invitation to serve as a Volunteer, the Peace Corps will send you a packet of information about your host country and a description of your pre-service training. The packet will include a recommended clothing packing list and a country-specific bibliography. Finally, you will receive reporting instructions with the date and location of your pre-departure orientation. The Peace Corps travel office will send you airline tickets, and soon you will be on your way to your country of service.

Some Suggestions to Help Speed Your Application Through the Peace Corps

- Make sure that you keep copies of all your application materials.
- Respond to all requests from the Peace Corps for additional legal and medical information as quickly as possible.
- Select your references from people who are readily available, and urge them to complete their forms as quickly as possible.
- Keep in touch, by phone or e-mail, with your recruiter and later your placement officer. Make sure you notify them of changes in your address or phone numbers.

Key Facts to Know About Serving as a Volunteer

- You must be at least eighteen years of age, in good health, and a U.S. citizen.
- There is no upper age limit.
- The length of service is two years.
- The Peace Corps is a U.S. government agency.

Redefine Online

You may still have some questions about what it is like to serve in the Peace Corps. Or you may be ready to fill out your Volunteer application now. Fortunately, it has never been easier to get the answers and apply online for the toughest job you will ever love. You can do both by logging on to the Peace Corps Web site at www.peacecorps.gov

Our Web site includes the most thorough and up-to-date information about serving as a Peace Corps Volunteer. You can learn more about urgent recruitment needs, Volunteer assignments, and the countries where Volunteers are serving. There is also a special section just for college students and information about diversity in the Peace Corps. Find out which universities offer graduate school opportunities through our Master's International and Fellows/USA programs. Or you can simply soak in the Peace Corps experience by reading more than fifty Volunteer stories, viewing photos, or downloading our free screensaver. Would you like to talk to someone about the Peace Corps? The Web site provides an up-to-date calendar of recruitment events nationwide, as well as information for contacting your regional recruitment office.

When you are ready to apply, the Web site is your pre-ferred destination. Complete and submit your Volunteer application and preliminary medical history on the Web. Our online Help section will guide you through the process, and there is no charge to apply. If you would like to download an application or have one mailed to you, simply fill out our online Application Request form.

Don't wait another minute to start the adventure of a lifetime.

Peace Corps Regional Offices

Atlanta, Georgia
(FL, GA, TN, MS, AL, SC, PR)
100 Alabama Street
Building 1924, Suite 2R70
Atlanta, GA 30303
(404) 562-3456
Fax (404) 562-3455
atlinfo@peacecorps.gov

Boston, Massachusetts
(MA, VT, NH, RI, ME)
10 Causeway Street
Room 450
Boston, MA 02222
(617) 565-5555
Fax (617) 565-5539
boston@peacecorps.gov

Chicago, Illinois
(IL, IN, MO, MI, OH, KY)
55 West Monroe Street
Suite 450
Chicago, IL 60603
(312) 353-4990
Fax (312) 353-4192
chicago@peacecorps.gov

Dallas, Texas
(TX, OK, LA, NM, AR)
207 South Houston Street
Room 527
Dallas, TX 75202
(214) 767-5435
Fax (214) 767-5483
dallas@peacecorps.gov

Denver, Colorado
(CO, KS, NE, UT, WY)
1999 Broadway
Suite 2205
Denver, CO 80202
(303) 844-7020
Fax (303) 844-7010
denver@peacecorps.gov

Los Angeles, California
(Southern CA, AZ)
11000 Wilshire Boulevard
Suite 8104
Los Angeles, CA 90024
(310) 235-7444
Fax (310) 235-7442
lainfo@peacecorps.gov

Minneapolis, Minnesota
(MN, WI, SD, ND, IA)
330 Second Avenue South
Suite 420
Minneapolis, MN 55401
(612) 348-1480
Fax (612) 348-1474
minneapolis@peacecorps.gov

New York, New York
(NY, NJ, CT, PA)
201 Varick Street
Suite 1025
New York, NY 10014
(212) 352-5440
Fax (212) 352-5441
nyinfo@peacecorps.gov

San Francisco, California
(Northern CA, NV, HI)
333 Market Street
Suite 600
San Francisco, CA 94105
(415) 977-8800
Fax (415) 977-8803
sfinfo@peacecorps.gov

Seattle, Washington
(WA, OR, ID, AK, MT)
2001 Sixth Avenue
Suite 1776
Seattle, WA 98121
(206) 553-5490
Fax (206) 553-2343
seattle@peacecorps.gov

Washington, D.C.
(DC, MD, NC, WV, DE, VA)
1525 Wilson Boulevard
Suite 250
Arlington, VA 22209
(703) 235-9191
Fax (703) 235-9189
dcinfo@peacecorps.gov

Headquarters
Peace Corps
Paul D. Coverdell Peace Corps Headquarters
1111 20th Street, NW
Washington, DC 20526
www.peacecorps.gov
(800) 424-8580